user-friendly
propHecy

Guidelines for the
Effective Use of Prophecy

Larry J. Randolph

Destiny Image® Publishers, Inc.
P.O. Box 310
Shippensburg, PA 17257-0310

"Speaking to the Purposes of God for this Generation
and for the Generations to Come"

ISBN 1-56043-695-6

For Worldwide Distribution
Printed in the U.S.A.

This book and all other Destiny Image, Revival Press,
and Treasure House books are available
at Christian bookstores and distributors worldwide.

For a U.S. bookstore nearest you, call **1-800-722-6774**.
For more information on foreign distributors, call **717-532-3040**.
Or reach us on the Internet: **http://www.reapernet.com**

Dedication

This book is gratefully dedicated to all the members of my family, especially Rebecca, my wife, who has always encouraged me to reach my potential in Christ. Her dedication and love for God and His Word have always been an inspiration to me—whether in everyday life, in the pulpit, or in the writing of this book. She is one of the most prophetic women I have ever known. I love her very much.

James, my father, has also played a vital role in my spiritual life. In addition to fathering me, he taught me to desire and respect spiritual gifts by modeling them for me.

Geraldine, my mother, has also been a wonderful example of a Christian who is laden with the fruits of the Spirit. By example, she taught me to love unconditionally and to be patient, gentle, forgiving, kind, and long-suffering.

Chris, Stephanie, Rene, Roland, and Jonathan—my five children—have also encouraged me in a way they may not know. Their understanding and acceptance of my calling has released me to travel throughout the Body of Christ, where I have birthed many of the principles presented in this book.

Also, thanks to all my grandchildren for being so wonderful. Thanks to my mother-in-law, Aurora, for all her prayers and support for me.

And a special thank you goes to my Lord Jesus Christ, whom I love with all my heart.

Endorsements

In a day when spiritual hyperbole often clouds and distorts the precious gifts given to the Church, it is good to see a book come along that accurately portrays the necessity of the Prophetic Gift. Larry has captured the power and simplicity, the elegance and crudeness, the Glory and the gory of the maturity process that turns the weak into the mighty through the Grace of Jesus Christ.

John Paul Jackson
Founder of Streams of Shiloh

Larry Randolph seems to clarify the mystery of the gift of prophecy in a way that is not theologically intimidating. I believe that this book will strengthen the faith and confidence of the Body of Christ in knowing how the Lord uses His prophets.

Tim Johnson
Former Washington Redskins Football Player

As one personally indebted to the Lord for Larry's prophetic ministry, it is a privilege to endorse his book, *User Friendly Prophecy*. It is a helpful and insightful work, and will serve to encourage, instruct, and bring prophetic release.

Dr. Guy Chevreau
Author of *Share the Fire*

Contents

Foreword

I find it quite ironic that I would be writing a foreword to a book on the subject of prophecy. Ironic, because until I met Larry Randolph, I was quite negative regarding the issue of prophecy. Or, it would be better to say I was quite negative in my view of "prophets." The only prophetic persons I knew were eccentric; one of them gave prophecies in parables and symbols, which were hard to understand.

I had been very skeptical of the prophetic emphasis in Kansas City in the late 1980s. I had been in the home of one of the prophetic personalities of the Kansas City Fellowship. In all honesty, part of my negative appraisal was the apparent excitement many people had regarding the prophetic. I was beginning to think that most people believed God had moved to Kansas City. My church was only about five hours away on the other side of Missouri. I was an insecure pastor who was threatened by the success and visibility of the church in Kansas City. I admit that I didn't really know Mike Bickel, but he is now one of my friends whom I have a great respect for and who is one of my important prayer partners.

So how did meeting Larry Randolph change my view of prophecy? It happened this way. John Arnott told me he wanted to introduce the prophetic into the meetings in Toronto where I was preaching at what was then called the Toronto Airport Vineyard Christian Fellowhip, now Toronto Airport Christian

Fellowship. I told him I didn't really want to, but I was in the role of the evangelist and would respect his decision. John invited Larry Randolph to come and minister since John's staff person, Mark Dupont, who was gifted prophetically, was out of the country at the time in Scandinavia.

We went to pick Larry up, and when I met him, I was initially very nervous about this prophetic person. How weird would he be? I found Larry to be very friendly and fun to be with. We talked some in the car on the way to the meeting. During the meeting I was praying for a pastor's wife who was having trouble breaking through into the Presence of God. I worked with her for a while, but to no avail. Then Larry stepped up by me and politely asked, "Would you care if I prayed for her? Perhaps God will give me some insight." I was frustrated and glad to have Larry take over since I was getting nowhere. It was like praying for a wall.

I watched as Larry asked the woman three questions. It was obvious that he knew more than he was sharing. In a brief period of time, the woman was in tears—no longer was she like praying for a brick wall. I was amazed at how natural Larry ministered, how gentle, how caring, how powerful was the effect. I was so impressed that I asked Larry to pray for me that I, too, might begin to prophesy over people like Larry had done. Larry prayed for me, and I still desire more anointing in the area of prophecy.

I was so impressed that I have had Larry join others to be one of the principal speakers at the last three prophetic conferences in my city, St. Louis. His times of sharing have been some of the most popular teachings given during these last three prophetic conferences. I think so much of Larry that I asked him to join my staff, but to no avail. God would not release him from his call to southern California. I consider him a dear friend and a man of integrity—a very nonreligious, yet spiritual person whom God raised up from the cotton fields of Arkansas and is using to touch His Church in this time. It is an honor to introduce Larry Randolph to you.

Randy Clark
Global Awakening Team Leader

Introduction

Over the last 20 years I have been asked both simple and complex questions concerning the gift of prophecy. Inquiring Christians have wanted to know such things as: Who can prophesy? What value does prophecy hold in the life of a believer? How do Christians know if they are called to a prophetic ministry?

In what manner do people receive and develop prophetic gifting? How do prophetic people relate to the Body of Christ and its leadership? And, most importantly, what is the proper use of prophecy in the twentieth-century Church?

Over the years, I have been able to satisfy the curiosity of casual seekers by giving brief and simple answers to their questions. For the most part, a great number of these people have taken my instruction to heart and have applied it to their lives and ministries. As a result, they seem better equipped to prophesy.

In the Church, however, there has always been a percentage of people who are not content with *simple* instruction. Many ordinary people have an *extraordinary* desire to understand the inner workings of spiritual gifting. This is especially true of prophetic people who have an insatiable hunger to know why, how, when, and where to use their gifts.

In response to this cry for deeper understanding, I have often prayed that someone would write a book addressing the many issues that surround the gift of prophecy and prophetic ministry.

I envisioned a book that was simple to read and easy to understand, but also in-depth and thorough. This book would be user-friendly, honest, filled with personal examples, and laced with humor. It would serve as a simple handbook, giving guidance to those who desire a greater insight into prophetic protocol and procedure. It would demystify the cloud of pseudo-spirituality that surrounds both prophecy and prophets. Most importantly, this book would bring a measure of credibility to a much-needed ministry gift—one that is so often misunderstood by the Church.

For several years I searched desperately for this kind of book. Although I came across a number of wonderful books on prophecy, I had yet to find what I had envisioned. Then it dawned on me! The book I was looking for is written upon the pages of my own heart. I had been reared in a prophetic environment and had given most of my life to prophetic ministry. So, why not share my own understanding of prophecy? After all, it was a burden that God had specifically given to me.

As a result of much soul searching, *User-Friendly Prophecy* was finally conceived. While accompanying me on a ministry trip to Scotland, my friend, Brian Bumpas, began to encourage me to commit my experience and knowledge of prophecy to writing. After returning, I spent the rest of that year writing and rewriting this book while lying on the floor of my office. When I was finished, Brian and I began to co-labor in the laborious task of revising the manuscript. Without his labor of love, I would not have created this book at this time. For this, I am most grateful.

By some standards, this manuscript may be lacking in eloquence and style. However, it is an honest and heartfelt book designed to equip an emerging generation of prophetic people—those believers who desire to edify, exhort, and comfort the Church through the gift of prophecy.

Part One

Establishing the Scriptural Validity of Prophecy

propHetic Heritage

My father quietly folded the newspaper he was reading and reached for his old blue coat. "Come on, son," he said. "We're going across town to see a car that's for sale." A split-second later, I was on my feet, following like a puppy behind its master.

"How much is the car?" I asked with curiosity. "Do you think we can afford it?"

With an all-knowing look that is common to my dad, he turned, smiled at me, and whispered, "The ad doesn't give the price, son, but I happen to know exactly what they are asking for it." Sure enough, when we arrived at the used-car lot, the salesman attempted to sell us the car for just the price my dad had told me.

Dad was right! In fact, Dad seemed to be right about most things. Whether it was the price of cars, a change in the weather, the names of unannounced dinner guests, or the secret sins of his own children, he seemed to have prior knowledge about things that he couldn't have known naturally. Where did Dad get this secret information? Some say he was clairvoyant or psychic. Neither of these described Dad. Instead, he was a simple, small-town preacher who was sensitive to the Spirit of God. His accurate impressions did not come from palmistry or fortune-telling, but were rooted in a conviction that God shares secrets with those who are His friends.

The denomination to which we belonged called such phenomena the "Spirit of Prophecy." Others acknowledged Dad's gift as the "word of knowledge" (see 1 Cor. 12:8). For the sake of those who struggle with the theology of spiritual gifting, let's just say that Dad was open to prophetic communication from God. He seemed to be tuned in to this frequency of spiritual perception at all times, and in spite of those within our denomination who believed that God speaks only within the confines of the church sanctuary, he exercised his gifting whenever and wherever necessary. He listened constantly for an inner witness that would direct him in the ordinary, everyday matters of life. His simple faith enabled him to cling to the notion that God not only lived in his heart, but also delighted in speaking to his mind.

Prophetic Environment

Growing up in a prophetic environment can be both frightening and unsettling to a young child. Yet, for me, it was as natural as the blue sky that hung over my boyhood home in Arkansas. Perhaps the reason I felt comfortable with supernatural gifts was my constant exposure to godly men and women throughout the formative years of my life.

As far back as I can remember, the exercise of supernatural giftings seemed to be a way of life for our family. In fact, some of my earliest memories are of hearing stories of miraculous events in the living room of our little house. Sitting on Grandpa's knees, I would listen to stories of our Uncle Newton who was a prophetic miracle worker in the early 1900s. With great conviction, Grandpa would recount the many healings worked on those who were blind, deaf, or crippled.

Occasionally, Dad would interrupt and relate how his own life had been spared by a warning in a dream. He would continue with recent examples of healings and visitations within the lives of our family members. As the evening wore on, other family members would join in with stories of other miracles—such as how my grandfather was saved from a premature death through the prayers of my father—other testimonies about healings, dreams, visions, and prophetic signs would evolve into a crescendo of high praise of the Lord. I remember the atmosphere being so charged with spiritual awareness that I was completely over-whelmed by the power of God's Presence. I would sit speechless, in awe of a sovereign God who responds to the simple faith of common people.

Chicken-Yard Prophecy

By the time I had entered grade school, I had developed an infatuation with the prophetic. Many nights, I would lie sleepless as I pondered the mysteries of the supernatural. Could *I* flow in the gifts of the Spirit? Would God use *me* in the ministry of the miraculous? These were the thoughts of a six-year-old boy, whose life was inspired by a great spiritual heritage, enriched by godly predecessors.

My first chance to test the prophetic gifting in my life came when I was in the first grade. On a cold winter morning, I awoke with a strange impression. I felt drawn to the chicken yard that lay behind our house. It seemed that I instinctively knew how many eggs our hens had laid the day before. I jumped out of bed and ran to the henhouse with great expectation. My heart pound-ed with excitement as I began to search the nests. I counted slowly—one, two, three, four, five. Right! I leaped with joy, thrilled because I had found the exact number of eggs that I had perceived would be there.

This incident might seem relatively insignificant to those who are spiritually mature; however, in my mind I had launched out on a journey into the realm of the prophetic. This chicken-yard prophecy was a small beginning, but from that day forward I had a sense that my gifting would someday develop into something of value and usefulness in God's Kingdom.

New York Prophecy

The year was 1977. As I stepped off the jumbo jet at La Guardia Airport in New York City, I was deep in thought, reflect-ing upon the past few decades of my life. More than 20 years had passed since my chicken-yard prophecy, and my prophetic gift-ing had grown considerably. Although I no longer knew how many eggs were in the henhouse, I was sure that God had placed a prophetic call on my life. I had determined to fulfill that call in a way that would be pleasing to God and beneficial to His people.

As I approached the crowd of unfamiliar faces in the airport terminal, I was perplexed. It seemed hard to believe, but I had just traveled over a thousand miles from my home in Arkansas in blind obedience to a prophetic dream that I had been given. Had I lost my mind, or was I operating with the mind of Christ? The implications of what I was doing began to slowly dawn upon me. Nevertheless, I was absolutely certain about three things.

First, earlier that month, I had a prophetic dream in which I was instructed to visit New York City. I was given no further information, other than seeing a vision of a white late-model car (which would later play a significant role in my trip). Second, in spite of the fact that I was broke, scared, and had never ventured out of my home state before—much less flown on a plane—I was determined to obey what I believed to be a prophetic word from the Lord. Third, out of obedience, I was now standing in a strange city, completely dependent upon God's leading and providence.

As I picked up the pay phone to summon a taxi, my mind began racing with all kinds of questions. *This faith and obedience stuff is great*, I thought, *but, now that I am here, what in the world am I going to do?*

I didn't know anyone on the East Coast, much less in New York City. I was totally alone, with no place to stay. To complicate matters, I had used all but $100 of my money to pay for the round-trip airline ticket. Even if God multiplied my money three-fold, I would neither be able to rent a hotel room nor buy enough food for the three days I was scheduled to be there.

In spite of my concerns, I squared my shoulders and put my best foot forward in faith. I boldly stepped into the awaiting taxi and asked the driver to take me to Stony Brook, Long Island, where I had heard that a Messianic conference was being held. Upon arrival, I randomly selected a hotel and used the remainder of my money to rent a room for the night. Clutching my last few dollars, I stumbled into the hotel café to have a cup of coffee and to ponder my strange predicament.

After being seated, I felt my faith start to waver as old doubts began to surface. *Why would God require such a thing from me anyway?* I mumbled. *Doesn't He care that I have no money to live on and no way to get back to the airport? Why am I here anyway? Have I missed God?* I sat still for a moment, awaiting an answer. When none came, I shrugged my shoulders in exasperation and turned to the only source of comfort I had at the moment—my cup of coffee.

As I sipped the warm coffee, I felt the Spirit of the Lord descend on me. Although I didn't know why, my attention was drawn to a man sitting at a table in the back of the restaurant. Middle-aged and well dressed, he seemed to be dining alone. At first, it appeared that this gentleman's attention was focused upon his food. However, as our eyes met, he seemed to lose interest in everything but our exchange of glances. Every few seconds, he would look up from his table and stare at me as if he desperately needed something.

What's wrong with this guy? I thought. *What does he want from me? And why do I feel sorry for him?* He didn't display any obvious signs of trouble or pain. Nor did there seem to be anything out of the ordinary about this man other than a rather melancholy expression on his face. Then, for the first time since I had left Arkansas, the Lord began to speak to me. He indicated that the man in the business suit was suicidal and that I was to go sit down beside him.

I was shocked! *No way, Lord! I was willing to brave flying in an airplane for the first time, even though I've been afraid of heights. I was willing to come to New York without provision, but I'm not going to make a fool out of myself in this restaurant! If You want me to speak to this man, You will have to have **him** approach **me**!*

Feeling confident that I was now off the hook, I quickly got into the line at the cash register to pay for my coffee. I had just stuck my change in my pocket when I felt a gentle tap on my right shoulder. At first I thought it was an impatient customer who was urging me to hurry out of the line. But much to my surprise, I heard a voice behind me saying, "Sir, are you a minister?" As I turned to see who had tapped my shoulder, I was dumbfounded. The gentleman whom the Lord had spoken to me about was now standing in front of me with a look of desperation upon his face.

I thought, *How did he know that I was a minister?* Till that day, I had neither seen nor talked to this man before. *Is this You, God? Would You bring me to New York to help **one** man?* With these thoughts swirling around in my mind, I followed the man back to his table, where he began to tell me about his life.

Richard

His name was Richard. He was raised Catholic, but rarely went to Mass. He believed in God; however, until recently, he had seen no reason to commit his life to the Lord. Prior to that year, he had a nice car, a beautiful wife, wonderful kids, and a partnership in a growing company. Everything seemed to be going his way until suddenly his world fell apart.

Approximately eight months before (much to the dismay of those who knew them both), his wife of many years had filed for a divorce. He had been asked to move out of his house and was forbidden to speak to his children. To add to this dilemma, his business began to falter. He had lost all hope and could not find a reason to live.

With great pain in his voice, Richard continued to tell me about the events leading up to our encounter. Two days prior to our meeting, he had left his home in Wisconsin to drive into New York to conduct business. In his mind, it was the last trip he would ever take. Once he had concluded his business, he was determined to kill himself with the gun he had stashed in the glove compartment of his car.

En route to New York, something significant had happened. He had tuned in his car radio to a gospel station where he heard

R.W. Shambach preach the message of salvation. For the first time in his life, Richard had decided to pray. "Lord, if You are really there and You care about me, I want to know. Otherwise, I am going to kill myself." At that point, he made an unusual request of the Lord. Almost reluctantly, he murmured, "God, if You will send someone to talk to me while I'm in New York, I will reconsider my plans."

Richard hesitated and then said to me, "That's why I approached you. I just had a feeling that you were a minister and could possibly help me. Are you the one? Can you really help me?"

As I struggled to control my heightened emotions, I paused briefly to gather my thoughts. Then, in faith, I opened my mouth, believing that God would give me the right thing to say. "Sir, I now know why I am in New York. Would you believe that God loves you so much that He would go to any lengths or extremes to help you? Would you believe that He would move Heaven and earth to divinely orchestrate our meeting? Would you also believe that our God is so extravagant that He would send an insignificant, small-town preacher all the way from Arkansas on a blind journey just to say, '*God loves you. **Please** don't take your life*'"?

With tears running down his face, Richard reached out and grabbed my hand. Looking directly into my eyes, he said, "What can I do to be saved? Will you come up to my hotel room and tell me more about the love of God?"

Without hesitating a moment, I responded, "Yes! God wants to save you and fill you with His Spirit."

Richard immediately responded to these words of hope and led me to his room where he encountered the living Lord. After several hours of talking, praying, and shedding tears of repentance, he was gloriously saved, delivered from his despair, and baptized in the Holy Spirit. Apparently, it had taken months for God to orchestrate this meeting, but in a matter of hours, a miracle had taken place. Richard's life was forever changed. He had found help in a God who was quick to respond to his cry of desperation.

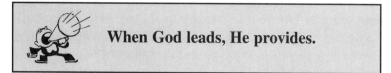

When God leads, He provides.

Now that God had met Richard's needs, my situation was also about to change. I would soon discover that when God leads, He provides. I had been willing for God to use me in Richard's life, and now this new believer had an intense desire to be a channel for *my* need. Richard felt impressed to buy my meals and pay my hotel bill for the remainder of my stay. In my eyes, it was a miracle of provision. I had been faithful to God, and He was now being faithful to me.

When it was time for me to return home, there was yet another blessing in store for me. Richard felt that he should drive me to the airport. When I saw his car, I was stunned. It was the same late-model white car I had seen in the prophetic dream that I received in Arkansas. Now I was seated in the front seat, conversing with the man whose prayer in this car had supernaturally interrupted my life and brought me to a place so far from home.

The Value of the Prophetic

That fall day in 1977 was the last time I laid eyes upon Richard. However, I often think about him and the lessons I learned through that experience. I thank God for the value of the prophetic. It is truly an endowment of God that is essential to the accomplishment of spiritual ministry. This instance in Richard's life seemed to demonstrate that an integral part of God's evangelistic outreach is carried out through prophetic ministry.

I also thank God for the grace and strength He gave me to obey His voice. My experience taught me that it is a great thing to receive a prophetic word, but an even greater act of spiritual maturity to obey that word. Had I not been obedient to prophetic instruction in Richard's case, he might have perished.

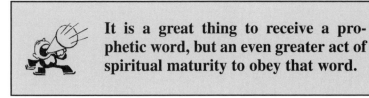

It is a great thing to receive a prophetic word, but an even greater act of spiritual maturity to obey that word.

Most of all, I'm thankful for the prophetic heritage that I received simply by being a member of a godly family. I remember with fondness how my father and grandfather encouraged me to memorize and recite Scriptures at an early age. I learned to value the written Word of God as a living training manual and historical workbook designed to equip and instruct the saints in the development of their prophetic gifts and callings. It is this understanding that has made it possible for me to properly develop my own prophetic gifting and has fostered a lifelong quest to gain biblical insight and understanding of the purpose and function of prophecy within the Body of Christ.

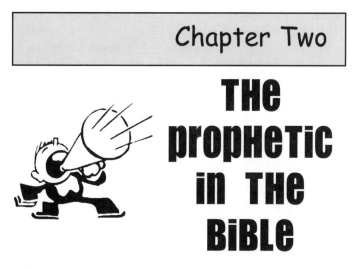

Chapter Two

THE PROPHETIC IN THE BIBLE

Life has shown me that people who are acknowledged as experts or masters within a specific field initially began by understanding the basics of that skill. This seems to be true of almost any trade, skill, or craft. Those who are accomplished in the art of music, acting, sports, etc., began by understanding the origin, history, and basic function of their crafts. For example, many acknowledge Jerry Rice as the greatest football receiver of all time. Television analysts, teammates, and coaches consistently point out that the key to his success is his commitment to drilling himself in the fundamentals of the sport. The pattern he runs and the spectacular plays he makes during a game are merely a reflex action, a conditioned response birthed by practicing the basics.

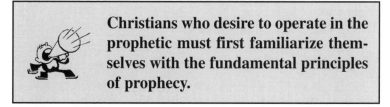

Christians who desire to operate in the prophetic must first familiarize themselves with the fundamental principles of prophecy.

This same standard applies to prophecy. Christians who desire to operate in the prophetic must first familiarize themselves with the fundamental principles of prophecy. Like artists and athletes, we must study the textbook, practice its principles, and play by the rules. As a result, we are able to gain mastery over the skills needed to accomplish prophetic ministry.

In view of this fact, then, is there a proper training manual for prophetic people? Without a doubt, the Bible is our text for prophecy. Every essential element we need to operate in the prophetic can be found in its pages. The Bible documents the role of the prophetic throughout the history of Israel and the early Church. And, like a football player who reviews the history of the game by studying the films of those who have played before him, we, too, can study and learn from the failure and success of the prophetic figures described in the Bible.

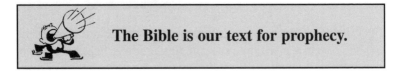

The Bible is our text for prophecy.

Biblical Overview of Prophecy

Several years ago I heard a pastor say, "I don't want the gift of prophecy operating in my church. I just want to stick to Jesus and the Bible." To some, this pastor's opinion might appear to be wise or, at least, worthy of consideration. Others would argue that his statement was born out of religious blindness and an ignorance of the Word of God. So, how do we know who is right? Are the "gift of prophecy" and "Jesus and the Bible" *mutually exclusive* as this pastor implies? Or, are the Spirit of Christ and the gift of prophecy *synonymous*?

Let's see what our text says.

We will begin by examining the existence of prophecy in the Bible. First, the words *prophet* and *prophets* are used nearly 600 times in the King James Version of the Bible. The words *prophecy*, *prophesy*, and *prophesied* are referred to more than 160 times in Old and New Testament passages of Scripture. In addition, Scripture makes many indirect references pertaining to the prophetic.

In light of these biblical references, we cannot ignore the existence of the prophetic in both the Old and New Testaments. From Genesis to Revelation, every book of the Bible is laden with prophetic implications. Beginning with the first page, God Himself set the precedent when He prophetically declared, "Let there be light." The last page of the Bible ends with an admonishment from Jesus to heed "the sayings of the prophecy of this book." Everything in between these two pages testifies to the fact that the prophetic is embedded deep within the fabric of Scripture.

> **From Genesis to Revelation, every book of the Bible is laden with prophetic implications.**

Emergence of Old Testament Prophets

According to the *Southwestern Pictorial Bible Dictionary*, page 685, prior to the prophets, all that Israel possessed in the form of God's will was the Law. The Lord had appeared to Moses on Mount Sinai where He gave the Ten Commandments as a guide for moral and ethical behavior. In addition to the tablets of stone containing the commandments, Moses later compiled a list of ordinances, rites, duties, rules, and regulations. He gave further guidance by writing the first five books of the Bible, known as the *Torah*. Once in possession of these guidelines, the people of God were expected to conduct their lives in a reasonable manner.

However, these laws did not specifically address many of the issues and situations that Israel would face. This did not come from any inherent weakness within the Law. Rather, it was simply impractical to address in detail every possible situation that would arise. Hence, the establishment of prophets in the Old Testament emerged from a great need to interpret the will of God for the nation of Israel. God met this need by granting revelation to these prophets. Their function was to bring specific revelation to issues not covered by the Law. God used their prophetic gifts to expose hidden sins, to find specific direction for His people, to defeat their enemies in battle, and to give personal prophetic words to both kings and commoners.

Since these prophets spoke into current situations, it is often said that they functioned as forth-tellers (speaking forth a current message), not foretellers (speaking of things to come). However, we must not forget that in many instances these prophets also spoke of the future—predicting both future blessings and calamities for the nation of Israel. For example, the prophet Isaiah spoke in beautiful language concerning the coming of the One who would save His people from their sins. Daniel, another Old Testament prophet, predicted the death of kings, the fall of future kingdoms, and also prophesied the approximate time of the Messiah's birth and ministry. These two prophets were spokesmen for their generation (forth-tellers) *and* prophetic seers (foretellers) who caught a glimpse of things that were yet to come.

Classification of Old Testament Prophets

The *Southwestern Pictorial Bible Dictionary* also states that the books in the Hebrew Old Testament can be divided into three parts: the Law, the Prophets, and the Writings. The Prophets category can be further subdivided into *former* and *latter prophets*. Under the heading of *former* prophets we find the Books of Joshua, First and Second Samuel, and First and Second Kings. The authors of these books are anonymous, but history indicates that they were men who held prophetic office in ancient Israel. Inspired by the Holy Spirit, they wrote a detailed history of the period prior to the *latter* prophets. (The term *latter* does not necessarily refer to chronological history, but is a label given to prophetic books that follow the former prophets in the Hebrew Old Testament.) Without this history, it would be impossible to understand the works of such men as Isaiah and other great spokesmen.

The *latter* prophets were also known as *writing* prophets. Included in this category are Isaiah, Jeremiah, and Ezekiel. These latter or writing prophets were not anonymous like the former prophets. They were called by God to deliver prophetic messages, not only to their own generation, but also for generations yet to come. Thus, their names were made known to establish their credibility to future generations. Scripture does not tell us how these men prepared their messages. However, it seems as though they were, first of all, public speakers and secondly, writers. Although Jeremiah 30:1-2 seems to demonstrate that this order is likely, it could be that in many instances these prophets enlarged and expounded upon their oral messages by writing them down.

Both the former and latter prophets had specific and complementary tasks to fulfill in the Old Testament. The former prophets set forth the history of a particular period in Israel's existence, while the latter prophets fulfilled parts of this history. Today their books stand as a testimony to the evidence of prophetic activity in the Old Testament.

Description of Various Old Testament Prophets

As indicated, there are various types of prophets found in the Old Testament. In theological terms, some of these men are given the title of *major* prophets, while others are designated as *minor* prophets. Some were well known for their ministry, while others seemed to be obscure. Yet, one thing is certain, like the colors in a rainbow, Old Testament prophets were as diverse in temperament as they were in calling. Living in different environments and in different epochs of history, they were unique in every expression of their lives and ministries.

Like the colors in a rainbow, Old Testament prophets were as diverse in temperament as they were in calling.

The historical background of these prophets varied from the poor to the rich, the ignorant to the educated, the weak to the strong, and the commoner to the aristocrat. In spite of this diversity, however, a common thread was woven throughout the tapestry of their lives. These prophets were all called by God and seemed to possess a willingness to fulfill that calling. Like Moses, the great prophet and deliverer, they were anointed by God to serve as His spokesmen to their generation.

Listed below, in chronological order, is a brief biographical sketch of these prophets.

1. ELIJAH—Was fed by birds and angels. He raised the dead and called fire down from Heaven.
2. ELISHA—Had a double portion of Elijah's spirit. He performed great miracles of healing and summoned angels.
3. JONAH—Had a prophetic ministry, which resulted in the entire population of Nineveh repenting and averting God's judgment.
4. AMOS—Was a colorful prophet who worked as a herdsman and rebuked Israel for idolatry.
5. HOSEA—Was a highly educated prophet with great spiritual vision, both allegorical and direct. God told him to marry a prostitute, named Gomer, as a sign.
6. JOEL—Prophesied the future outpouring of God's Spirit upon all flesh, cited by Peter in the Book of Acts.
7. ISAIAH—Was one of the most prolific prophets. He foretold the coming of the Messiah. He is referred to as the *evangelist* of the Old Testament.
8. MICAH—Prophetically spoke judgment as well as Messianic prophecy to Israel.
9. OBADIAH—Is commonly described as a *minor* prophet who predicted the destruction of Edom.
10. NAHUM—Is acknowledged as a poetic prophet whose book some call a literary masterpiece. He also predicted the destruction of Nineveh.
11. JEREMIAH—Was a compassionate prophet who is known as the "weeping prophet." His writings were known as a book of prophetic sermons.
12. HABAKKUK—Was possibly a Levitical musician. He prophesied utilizing a lyrical form.
13. ZEPHANIAH—Was a prophet of royal descent who held a prominent position within the nation.

14. DANIEL—Was endowed with great wisdom, understanding, and discernment. He received and interpreted dreams, and he had apocalyptic visions.
15. EZEKIEL—Was a powerful preacher who was both priest and prophet. He received many unusual visions and was commanded to dispense the prophetic in an equally unusual way. A great portion of his writings were prophecies relating to the restoration of the nation of Israel.
16. ZECHARIAH—Was a priest and prophet who prophesied the destruction and restoration of Jerusalem. His writings consisted of eight symbolic visions.
17. HAGGAI—Prophesied the rebuilding of God's Temple, declaring that its latter glory would be far greater than its former glory.
18. MALACHI—Was sent to correct the Levites, restore the Law, and declare that "Elijah" (John the Baptist) would come before the great and terrible day of the Lord.

The School of the Prophets

The Old Testament also briefly mentions other prophets. Again, the *Southwestern Pictorial Bible Dictionary*, page 687, states that when the people of Israel entered the Promised Land, they rejected God as their ruler and decided that they must have a king (see 1 Sam. 8:4-7). In compliance with Israel's demand, God gave them a king. However, the first king, Saul, was not a man after God's own heart, but was concerned with his own welfare. To further complicate matters, at the time of Saul's reign, Israel was endangered by the idolatry of Canaan and the militaristic advances of the Philistines. Therefore, for the spiritual welfare of the nation, God raised up several companies, or "schools of the prophets." Not much is known about them, but it is assumed that this band of prophets spoke the word of God to the leaders of their day (see 1 Sam. 19:19-20; 2 Kings 2:3-5).

The Bible doesn't tell us if the "school of the prophets" was a formal organization. However, many scholars believe that these prophetic groups of people were initially knit together serving under the supervision of the prophet Samuel. Although it cannot be positively stated that Samuel was the founder of these groups, such an assumption would seem to have much in its favor—especially if you consider that the phrase, "School of the Prophets," originated and flourished during the life of this great prophet.

Also, following Samuel's death, these prophetic bands seemed to disappear until the times of Elijah and Elisha, where they suddenly appeared again, bearing the title: *sons of the prophets* (see 1 Kings 20:35). Apparently, this phrase revealed the close association between these groups of prophets and their relationship to Elijah and Elisha. After this, we hear no more about the company of the prophets. It appears that other prophetic men who followed them in biblical history were inclined to minister alone.

New Testament Prophets

In the same way that prophets and prophecy thrived in the Old Testament era, they also flourished throughout the New Testament. In the Book of Luke, Zacharias prophesied that his son, John the Baptist, would be called a prophet, preparing the way of the Messiah. Years later, John would fulfill this prophecy and be recognized by his contemporaries as a major prophet. Jesus verified this claim by stating that John the Baptist was the greatest prophet who ever lived. Afterward, our Lord also declared Himself to be a prophet, fulfilling Moses' prediction that the Messiah would come in the office of a prophet to deliver Israel. (See Luke 1:76; 7:26,28; 13:33.)

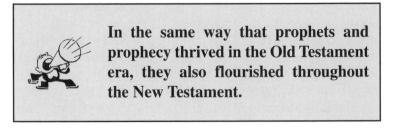

In the same way that prophets and prophecy thrived in the Old Testament era, they also flourished throughout the New Testament.

Both John the Baptist and Jesus exemplify the biblical model of a prophet. However, the prophet Joel had foretold a time when the gift of prophecy would be given to all believers. We see this word fulfilled on the day of Pentecost. The Spirit descended, and now all of God's people have the opportunity to be prophetic, for the gift was given to sons and daughters of Israel. (See Joel 2:28-29; Acts 2:17.)

As a result of this prophetic outpouring, according to the *Southwestern Pictorial Bible Dictionary*, page 267, many things occurred. As the New Testament Church matured, a diversity of gifts quickly emerged. A great number of individuals were bestowed with a special power of utterance, while others gravitated toward a ministry equal to the status of a prophet (see 1 Cor. 12:10). Therefore, it would be correct to say that all who spoke *the word of the Lord* were prophetic; whereas, others were further distinguished in order that they might bear the prophet's mantle.

One such man was the apostle Paul. He was recognized as a prophet, in addition to being an apostle and teacher. The distinction between his prophetic ministry and the other two offices he held were as follows: While the apostle is a *sent one* who establishes and builds the Church, *the prophet is a messenger to the Church.* Whereas the teacher explains and enforces biblical truth, *the prophet is recognized by his hearers as a divine channel of fresh revelation.* (Note: This revelation is not extra-biblical revelation, but fresh light brought upon biblical truth.)

In addition to Paul, several other New Testament prophets are specifically identified in Scripture. Judas and Silas were prophets at Antioch. Agabus and other prophets resided in Jerusalem. Philip the evangelist had four daughters who were highly prophetic. Others were also found moving from church to church to speak the word of the Lord. (See Acts 11:27-28; 15:32; 21:9.)

There also was another man who was endowed with such literary prowess that he committed his visions and revelations to writing. He is known as John the Revelator. Like Ezekiel in the Old Testament, this prophet/apostle recorded the revelation he received on the Isle of Patmos into what has become our Book of Revelation. This prophetic masterpiece is so profound that men of all religious persuasions acknowledge John as a true prophet.

Jesus the Prophet

As indicated, there are many Christians who do not associate Jesus and the Bible with the spirit of prophecy. Yet, to acknowledge Jesus in Scripture is to acknowledge prophecy. Revelation 19:10 states that *the testimony of Jesus is the spirit of prophecy.* He is the embodiment of the prophetic. Thousands of years before His birth, Moses spoke of His prophetic nature, saying, "The Lord thy God will raise up unto thee a Prophet from the midst of thee, of thy brethren, like unto me; unto Him ye shall hearken" (Deut. 18:15).

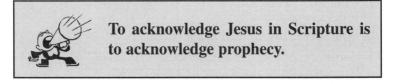

To acknowledge Jesus in Scripture is to acknowledge prophecy.

A close look at the life and ministry of Jesus will verify this prophecy spoken by Moses. Jesus, who was considered a prophet by most of His contemporaries, fulfilled prophecy, prophesied future events, and flowed in the ministry of personal prophecy. In fact, every word spoken by our Lord Jesus was pregnant with prophetic implications.

For instance, there are dozens of references to Jesus' personal prophetic ministry in the four Gospels. In John 1:48, He had revelatory knowledge concerning the whereabouts of Nathanael. In other passages of Scripture, He had prophetic insight into the hidden motives of Peter's heart and perceived the colorful past of a Samaritan woman. Prior to resurrecting his friend, Lazarus, He prophesied to the disciples and then again to Mary and Martha that Lazarus would rise from the dead as a testimony to God's power over death. (See Matthew 26:31-35; John 4:16-19; 11:1-16.) Jesus also knew the evil thoughts of the Pharisees and foresaw the treachery of Judas. And, toward the end of His ministry, He foretold the destruction of Jerusalem and predicted the exact details of His own death and resurrection.

Finally, as revealed in the Book of Revelation, since His ascension, Jesus has continued to function in His role as Prophet to the Church, exhorting and comforting His Bride. And we, too, are encouraged by His Spirit, through the apostle Paul, to "desire spiritual gifts, but rather that ye may **_prophesy_**. ... For ye may all prophesy one by one, that all may learn, and all may be comforted" (1 Cor. 14:1,31; see also Mt. 12:40; Lk. 11:17; 21:20-24; Jn. 12:32; 13:27).

Summary

It should be evident from the previous examples that Scripture validates prophetic ministry. It should also be clear that the Bible is a wonderful textbook from which we can learn the fundamentals of the prophetic, and when we establish our prophetic ministries in compliance with Scripture, we minimize the possibility of failing in the development of our skill.

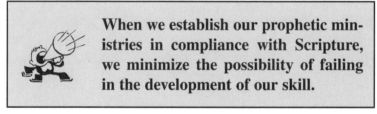

When we establish our prophetic ministries in compliance with Scripture, we minimize the possibility of failing in the development of our skill.

However, in addition to understanding the historical background and basic function of prophecy in the Bible, we must address several other issues. What is the essence of prophecy today? How do we receive the gift of prophecy? Does it come to us through grace or works? And, finally, how do we administrate the gift of prophecy? In the next chapter I will attempt to answer these questions.

Chapter Three

THE GifT Of propHecy

Now concerning spiritual gifts, brethren, I would not have you ignorant (1 Corinthians 12:1).

The very nature of the word *gift* implies that something has been freely given, without cost or expense. The Bible states in Romans 8:32 that God will "freely give us all things." The same is true of the "nine gifts of the Spirit," found in First Corinthians 12:8-10. In this portion of Scripture, the apostle Paul declares that the word of wisdom, word of knowledge, faith, healings, miracles, prophecy, discerning of spirits, tongues, and interpretation of tongues are given by the Holy Spirit as He (the Spirit) sees fit. The implications are clear. We cannot buy, bargain for, or earn the gifts of the Spirit. They are endowments of God and are imparted to His children—free of charge.

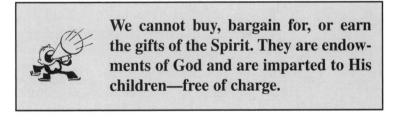

We cannot buy, bargain for, or earn the gifts of the Spirit. They are endowments of God and are imparted to His children—free of charge.

The truth of God's free gift was made real to me as a young man. In the early 1970s, I had two friends who possessed a strong desire to receive and administer the gift of prophecy. Each had sensed that he would one day minister this endowment to the Church; however, neither of them knew how to receive or appropriate the gift.

Driven by a passion to receive this gifting, one of my friends, who was unemployed, began to give himself to seasons of prayer and fasting. Periodically, he would spend days and weeks on his face before the Lord, crying out for impartation.

My second friend, on the other hand, trusted the desires of his heart to God and continued to work a job, raise a family, and minister part-time. His busy schedule allowed him very little time to launch an all-out assault on the throne of God. Other than occasional fasting and periodic seasons of prayer, he just "faithed it," believing that God's gift comes as a result of His grace.

Many years have passed since those days, and an amazing thing has happened. In spite of the different methods employed by my two friends, they are both presently flowing in the gift that they desired. I am convinced that one friend received his gift not because of a dedication to "*pray it in*," but because of God's sovereign choice. Likewise, my other friend's inability to pursue the gift of prophecy through prayer and fasting did not disqualify him from freely receiving it. Thus, time proved to me what theory could only suggest: The impartation of spiritual gifts is not dependent upon performance or pressure from men.

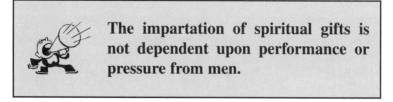

The impartation of spiritual gifts is not dependent upon performance or pressure from men.

The Gifts of the Spirit in First Corinthians

The spiritual gifts found in First Corinthians 12:8-10 can be divided into three categories: power gifts, revelation gifts, and utterance gifts.

1. Power gifts include:
   a. *Working of miracles:* the ability to perform supernatural signs and wonders.
   b. *Gifts of healing:* the ability to cure various kinds of ailments and diseases.
   c. *Faith:* the ability to act like God in "calling those things that are not as though they are" (see Rom. 4:17).
2. Revelation gifts include:
   a. *Word of wisdom:* the ability to discern and declare the proper wisdom for a person or situation.
   b. *Word of knowledge:* the ability to discern and declare things known to others but unknown to you at the time.
   c. *Discerning of spirits:* the ability to discern the presence of spirits, both good and bad.
3. Utterance gifts include:
   a. *Tongues:* the ability to speak an unlearned tongue or dialect.
   b. *Interpretation of tongues:* the ability to translate an unlearned tongue or dialect.
   c. *Prophecy:* the ability to see and predict the future; also to declare the revealed word of God.

Although all nine of these gifts are vital to the Body of Christ, Paul seemed to highlight the gift of prophecy in his writings to the Corinthian church. In First Corinthians 14:1 he writes, "…desire spiritual gifts, but rather that ye may prophesy." Two things are apparent in this Scripture. First, there is an understanding that the believer has access to all spiritual gifts; otherwise, we would not be encouraged to desire something we couldn't have. Second, Paul, by the inspiration of the Holy Spirit, singles out prophecy and gives it priority over the other gifts. He further stresses the importance of this gift by declaring in verse 5, "…greater is he that prophesieth…."

In light of the importance given to prophecy in these two Scriptures, and in keeping with the prophetic theme of this book,

I want to focus solely upon the gift of prophecy. However, any attempt to define prophecy is greatly complicated by the two revelation gifts—the word of wisdom and the word of knowledge—which overlap and blend with the gift of prophecy. In many instances, all three of these gifts flow together in a prophetic stream, making it difficult to distinguish one from the other. Yet, in spite of their compatibility to prophecy, we will not define the word of knowledge and the word of wisdom in this chapter. Our priority is prophecy; our goal is to understand its use.

Prophecy Defined

Over the years many people have asked me the question, *"What is prophecy and how do we flow in it?"* I always answer this question by beginning with the basics. I tell them that the *Strong's Exhaustive Concordance of the Bible* defines the Greek words *propheteis* and *prophetcuo* (prophecy and prophesy) in this manner: "to predict, to foretell, to speak under inspiration."

I also instruct them that in the *Scribner's Dictionary of the Bible*, the word most frequently used to describe prophecy in the Old Testament is *nabi*. This Hebrew word is used over 300 times and is long associated with a root that means to "bubble up." It is now more usually connected with a kindred Arabic word meaning " to announce." References, such as *Irwin's Bible Commentary*, verify this by interpreting prophecy as, "the declaring of God's will, whether for the present or the future." In *Scribner's Dictionary of the Bible*, prophecy is described as, "authoritative announcement of the Divine will in a particular case."

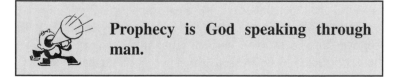

Prophecy is God speaking through man.

Undoubtedly, there are many other valid references that accurately define the meaning of prophecy. Yet all of these definitions can be reduced to one simple thought: *Prophecy is God speaking through man*. This truth is substantiated in 430 instances throughout the Old Testament where prophetic figures declared, "Thus saith the Lord." Peter exemplifies this dynamic in the New Testament by writing, "If any man speak, let him speak as the oracles of God..." (1 Pet. 4:11).

Unique Characteristics of the Gift of Prophecy

Undoubtedly, it is a great honor to speak for the Lord. However, before God can use us as His mouthpiece, we must understand two characteristics unique to the gift of prophecy. First, there is a requirement that we must fulfill, which is the baptism of the Holy Spirit. Second, it appears that once New Testament believers have received the infilling of the Spirit, the gift of prophecy lies resident within them. As a result of this abiding anointing, we have the capacity to prophesy when and where the Spirit desires us to speak.

To better understand these dynamics, let's examine for a minute the first principle, which states that the baptism of the Spirit precedes the gifts of the Spirit in a believer's life. This dynamic is clearly demonstrated in Acts 19:1-6. Paul asked the Christians at Ephesus, "Did you receive the Holy Spirit when you believed?"

They said, "No, we have not even heard that there is a Holy Spirit." When Paul laid his hands upon them, the Holy Spirit came upon them, and they spoke with tongues and prophesied. Thus, it's apparent from this portion of Scripture that you can be a believer but not yet possess the baptism of the Holy Spirit.

In addition to Acts 19, several other New Testament Scriptures promote the concept of Spirit baptism before the gifts. In Luke 1:67, Zacharias, the father of John the Baptist, was filled with the Holy Spirit and prophesied. In Acts 2:1-36, Peter descended from the Upper Room on the day of Pentecost and, being freshly baptized in the Spirit, prophesied from the Book of Joel. Please understand: They flowed in prophecy only after receiving the Holy Spirit as a second experience to salvation. The formula was: salvation + baptism of the Spirit = an open channel for prophecy to flow.

Now, let's look at the second principle, which we will call the *resident anointing*. For those who have received the infilling of the Spirit, this dynamic enables them to draw at all times upon the gift that dwells within their spirits.

For instance, Old Testament prophecy came as a result of outward stimulation; whereas, the New Testament gift operates as a result of an inward witness and inner prompting of the Holy Spirit. The one is an anointing coming *upon us* (Old Testament). The other is an anointing dwelling *within us* (New Testament). This contrast between the Old Testament and the New Testament anointing is made apparent in the following Scriptures.

Old Testament: "The spirit rested *upon* them" (Num. 11:25).
New Testament: "Christ *in* you, the hope of glory" (Col. 1:27).

Old Testament: "I have put My spirit *upon* Him" (Is. 42:1).
New Testament: "Christ may dwell *in* your hearts" (Eph. 3:17).

Old Testament: "Word of the Lord came *unto* me" (Ezek. 6:1).
New Testament: "Word of Christ dwell *in* you" (Col. 3:16).

Old Testament: "Spirit of the Lord fell *upon* me" (Ezek. 11:5).
New Testament: "They were all *filled* with the Holy Ghost" (Acts 2:4).

Old Testament: "The spirit of the Lord God is *upon* Me" (Is. 61:1).
New Testament: "The anointing...abideth *in* you" (1 Jn. 2:27).

Old Testament: "Spirit of Elijah doth rest *on*" (2 Kings 2:15).
New Testament: "Spirit of truth...shall be *in* you" (Jn. 14:17).

In light of these Scriptures, it could be said that the same anointing that rested *upon* the prophets of old is now resident *within* the believer. Unlike our spiritual forefathers, we—as Spirit-filled Christians—are not limited to relying solely upon an external manifestation of God's Spirit. Instead, we can look to the well of living water that resides within us and, at any time, apply it to the need. Whether it be discernment, healing, prophecy, wisdom, or knowledge, the manifestation will come from the Christ who lives in us, not the Christ who is seated above us.

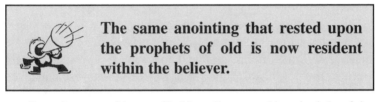

The same anointing that rested upon the prophets of old is now resident within the believer.

Over the years, I have relied heavily upon this principle of the *abiding anointing*. However, I came by this lesson the hard way. Before learning to appropriate the *gift within*, I spent a lot of time in prayer and fasting. My expectation was for the Spirit of God to fall upon me and give me direction. I can remember kneeling on my knees awaiting a sign from Heaven—something like a vision, an angel, or an audible voice from God. I was determined to receive my word from God in the natural realm of sight, touch, or sound.

In spite of my persistence, however, nothing tangible ever seemed to manifest. Weary and frustrated, I would finally give up and go about my everyday business. Then, much to my surprise, the word I so desperately needed would begin to arise out of the depths of my spirit. It seemed that I had an inner witness confirming what I should do and where I should go. I soon learned that my answers seldom came by way of outer manifestations. Instead, they came out of the *ever abiding word of the Lord* that lived within me. I began to trust this inner witness, as opposed to relying upon outward manifestations in the realm of sight, sound, and touch.

Don't get me wrong. In spite of the fact that God chose not to reveal Himself to me in a visible or audible way, I didn't abandon my pursuit of God through prayer and fasting. In fact, I strongly believe that prayer dials down the clamor of our soul and heightens our ability to hear and be led by the inner witness of the Holy Spirit. As previously mentioned, we do not buy God's Spirit or His gifts with acts of service. At the same time, these spiritual exercises can contribute to the awareness and manifestation of His anointing that is resident within us.

A Step Beyond

It's one thing to recognize the abiding gift of prophecy and yet another to use it accurately and precisely. As believers, we must be sensitive to this issue and endeavor to represent, as best we can, the true heart of the Lord. Before we express ourselves prophetically, we need to be aware that we are speaking for a God who is complex in nature, advanced in communication, and shrouded with mystery.

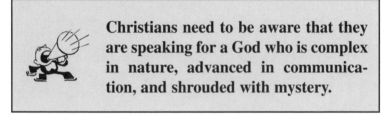

Christians need to be aware that they are speaking for a God who is complex in nature, advanced in communication, and shrouded with mystery.

To exercise this kind of prophetic utterance, which is a step beyond the First Corinthians 12:10 gift of prophecy, a few things are necessary. To begin, we must understand that we are faced with the difficulty of representing a God whom we hardly know or understand. Although the development of this skill is not yet necessary for young believers who operate in a beginner's level of prophecy, it is absolutely essential for maturing prophets. Those who flow in deeper dimensions of prophetic expression should know that more is required of those "who have been given much" (see Lk. 12:48).

Over the years, I have spent countless hours meditating upon the inherent difficulty of this task. How can we, with any degree of accuracy, articulate the heart of a God whom we cannot see or touch? Futhermore, if prophecy is the vehicle by which we express the thoughts of God, then how can we translate into human dialect what we receive from God? I concluded that without the help of the Holy Spirit, any attempt to capture the heart of God in human language would be like trying to thread the universe through the eye of a needle.

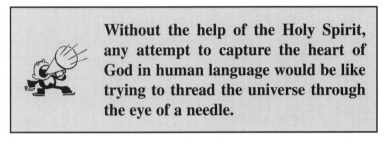

Without the help of the Holy Spirit, any attempt to capture the heart of God in human language would be like trying to thread the universe through the eye of a needle.

I also embraced the undeniable truth that God is a spiritual entity, not a human being. His ways are not our ways, neither are His thoughts our thoughts (see Is. 55:8). He does not think like a human, act like a human, or live in the realm of human experience. His first language is not English, German, Spanish, French, or any other kind of earthly tongue. It's true that He often converses with us on a human level, but, in reality, He is capable of communicating in a form far above and beyond the realm of human thought or articulation. In a split second, He can convey by His Spirit more information than we could enunciate in a thousand years. The apostle Paul testifies to this truth in Second Corinthians 12:2-4 (TLB):

Fourteen years ago I was taken up to heaven for a visit. Don't ask me whether my body was there or just my spirit, for I don't know; only God can answer that. But anyway, there I was in paradise, and heard things so astounding that they are beyond a man's power to describe or put in words....

Reception vs. Perception

Now that we are aware of the difficulty of expressing spiritual things with the human tongue, how then do we flow in our resident gift of prophecy? To begin, we must understand the difference between Old and New Testament prophecy. A greater part of Old Testament prophecy is *revelation received*; whereas, much of New Testament prophecy is *revelation perceived*. Both are inspired by God, but each exists within a different dispensation of time. One is before Christ, the other after Christ.

For example, Old Testament prophets declared, "Thus saith the Lord," over and over again. They seemed to repeat, word for word, audible statements spoken to them by God in their own language. However, there isn't one instance in the New Testament where believers said, "Thus saith the Lord." True, God did speak to many New Covenant prophets in the first century Church, but the absence of a "Thus saith the Lord" seemed to indicate a different kind of prophetic flow. Apparently, a measure of spiritual sensing and perception was involved in their lives and ministry. Expressions like, "and this I speak...and I think also that I have the Spirit of God," or "it seemed good to the Holy Ghost, and to us," or "the Spirit speaketh expressly," and "I say the truth in Christ...my conscience also bearing me witness in the Holy Ghost" appeared to be the rule for prophetic expression in the New Testament Church (see 1 Cor. 7:35,40; Acts 15:28; 1 Tim. 4:1; Rom. 9:1).

The New Testament "gift of prophecy" carries with it the privilege of interpreting the thought and intent of God's heart. ... We, as believers under the New Covenant, have a greater latitude of expression than did our Old Testament counterparts.

In light of these Scriptures, it is apparent that the New Testament "gift of prophecy" carries with it the privilege of interpreting the thought and intent of God's heart. It is not merely the act of repeating exact statements as dictated by God in the Old Testament (*revelation received*). Rather, it is the ability to perceive God's heart and articulate it (*revelation perceived*). Initially the thought will come from God, but through the process of translation it will be filtered through our culture, intellect, language, and personality.

It would be unwise to speak for God until we have become His friend.

Finally, the most significant difference between *revelation received* and *revelation perceived* is that we, as believers under the New Covenant, have a greater latitude of expression than did our Old Testament counterparts. Even so, this freedom comes as a result of an intimate relationship with the Lord. And, if we fail to develop that intimacy, we run the risk of misinterpreting or misrepresenting His heart—in which case, it would be unwise to speak for God until we have become His friend.

God's Humble Mouthpiece

On the other hand, those of us who are friends with Jesus must believe that our thoughts, hearts, and tongues are inspired by the Spirit of God. As a result of this intimacy with the Lord, we are capable of imparting the prophetic in a manner that is independent of our own self-righteousness. Why? In spite of our

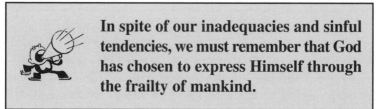

In spite of our inadequacies and sinful tendencies, we must remember that God has chosen to express Himself through the frailty of mankind.

inadequacies and sinful tendencies, we must remember that God has chosen to express Himself through the frailty of mankind, especially those who are joined to Him in relationship.

*For it was not through any human whim that man prophesied of old; **men they were**, but, impelled by the Holy Spirit, they spoke the words of God* (2 Peter 1:21 NEB).

Now, I know that I, too, am just a man, and I am also aware of the difficulty of expressing God's fullness with the human tongue. I know in part and I prophesy in part. However, in spite of all these limitations, I am still able to flow in a legitimate form of the prophetic. I prophesy not because I'm perfect, but because of His perfect word, which is within me.

Furthermore, I hardly ever attempt to speak a prophetic word to people without using words like, *I perceive*, *I sense*, or *I discern*. Seldom do I say, "Thus saith the Lord," or repeat a preprogrammed word. I have learned that we are not prophetic puppets on a string. Instead, we are the children of God, learning to interpret the heart of our Father and express it the best we can. We are uniquely different from other prophetic figures and are original in our delivery. When prophesying, it may be our mouth, our voice, and our words, but the inspiration comes from God and is birthed out of intimacy with Him.

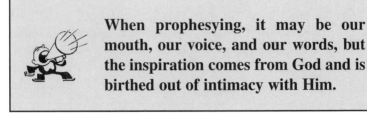

When prophesying, it may be our mouth, our voice, and our words, but the inspiration comes from God and is birthed out of intimacy with Him.

In view of this relationship with Christ, are we free to prophetically express ourselves as we choose? Absolutely not! It would be a great mistake to presume that God would validate every word that we speak. Neither will He bless those who prophesy anything that pops into their heads. Occasionally, we may accidentally stumble onto the word of the Lord, but bear in mind, mature prophecy is a skill that is developed by those who spend time with God. So, get to know God and you will find that He is eager to reveal the hidden things of His heart to you. Remember, friends tell friends secrets.

Chapter Four

propHecy— THe greater gifT

I wish you all had the gift of "speaking in tongues" but, even more, I wish you were all able to prophesy, preaching God's messages, for that is a greater and more useful power than to speak in unknown languages... (1 Corinthians 14:5 TLB).

In the last chapter we determined that prophecy is an endowment to the Church—a free gift from God. We learned that prophecy is God speaking through man and that the New Testament gift of prophecy is resident within the believer. We also determined that exercising this gift under the New Covenant gives us the privilege of interpreting the thought and intent of God's heart. However, it's one thing to understand the definition and use of prophecy and yet another thing to understand the significance of its role in the Church. Therefore, a question of priority arises. Does prophecy have a greater value than the other nine gifts of the Spirit, and is it a greater thing to prophesy than to speak with tongues?

Childhood Observations

As a young child, I spent hundreds of hours sitting in the pews of our little church. There were times when I was just plain bored and other times when I was captivated by the moving of the Holy Spirit. During those times of spiritual outpouring, I was perched on my seat, like a bird on a wire. With intense curiosity,

I observed the manifestation of spiritual gifts as they surfaced within the meetings.

On those occasions when God chose to manifest Himself, people would be saved, healed, and baptized in the Spirit. During these times, certain members of the church would become overly excited about what was happening and burst forth in a strange language, known as the "gift of tongues." Then, everything would stop as people bowed their heads in awe of an utterance from God.

At the time, I was unable to understand the importance our congregation attached to these strange tongues. However, I learned to accept them. What choice did I have? I was told that the public expression of tongues during the service was God speaking to the church. If that were true, I thought, then who was I to contend with the Almighty? If He wished to speak in gibberish, then I supposed that I should listen. Yet, I could never figure out why God would talk to me in a language I could not understand.

Tongues in Context

There is an amazing quality that resides within the heart of most children. They seem to have a sixth sense that enables them to navigate through the treacherous waters of fallacious thinking. Adults may be fooled indefinitely, but children seem to know when things are not quite right. They may not fully understand what they are sensing, nor can they articulate it, but later in life they find out that the uneasy feelings within their hearts was nothing less than discernment in its purest form.

The same was true of my experience with the use of tongues in our little church. I had no theology to support my gut feeling, but I knew there was more to God's voice than a vague utterance in unknown tongues. I suspected that a God who could speak in any language would not limit Himself to only one form of communication.

Don't get me wrong. I believe in speaking in tongues and appreciate its place in the Christian experience. However, I am convinced, like the apostle Paul, that tongues must be used in a way that is beneficial for the Church.

> *Even in the case of inanimate objects which are capable of making sound, such as a flute or harp, unless their notes have the proper intervals, who can tell what tune is being played on them?...So, in your case, unless you make intelligible sounds with your "tongue" how can anyone know what you are talking about? You might just as well be addressing an empty room!* (1 Corinthians 14:7-9 PME)

What is Paul saying? Is he suggesting there is no value to speaking in tongues? No, in fact he validates tongues by charging the church to "*Forbid not to speak with tongues*" (1 Cor. 14:39). Speaking out of personal experience, he also said, "I thank my God, I speak with tongues more than ye all" (1 Cor. 14:18). So, Paul's contention was not with tongues, per se, but with the misuse of them in public meetings, especially when there is no interpretation for the tongue spoken. That is the reason he pleaded with those who spoke in tongues to pray that they may interpret (1 Cor 14:13).

Setting Order

According to the Scriptures just mentioned, there was obviously a misuse of tongues within the Corinthian church. The outpouring of the Spirit had impacted the believers in such a way that most were overcome with a feverish desire to exercise their gifts publicly. As a result, the Corinthians began to speak in tongues simultaneously, leaving very little room for interpretation. Knowing the confusion that was created by these ecstatic utterances, Paul was faced with the task of "setting divine order."

Paul's concern was twofold. First, how could he encourage the operation of this gift and at the same time prevent the mass confusion that arose as a result of overzealous tongue-talkers? Second, was it possible to convince the unbelievers who were present as to the validity of "spiritual gifts"?

Paul demonstrated his wisdom and apostolic authority when he proclaimed a simple solution to this complex problem in Corinth. Concerning the first issue he wrote:

If the question of speaking with a "tongue" arises, confine the speaking to two or three at the most. They must speak in turn and have someone to interpret what is said. If you have no interpreter then let the speaker with a "tongue" keep silent in the church and speak only to himself and God (1 Corinthians 14:27-28 PME).

Paul clarifies the remaining issue in this manner:

So if the whole congregation is assembled and all are using the "strange tongues" of ecstasy, and some unin-structed persons or unbelievers should enter, will they not think you are mad? But if all are uttering prophecies, the visitor, when he enters, hears from everyone something that searches his conscience and brings conviction, and the secrets of his heart are laid bare. So he will fall down and worship God, crying "God is certainly among you!" (1 Corinthians 14:23-25 NEB)

Inspiration vs. Information

Just because a word is *inspirational*, doesn't mean that it's *informational*. The same is true of an utterance in tongues that is not accompanied with an interpretation. In many instances, an unintelligible expression in tongues can inspire our spirit and soul, but all too often our minds are left in the dark. Therefore, to minister to the whole man, both of these dynamics are essential. There must be information for the mind and inspiration for the spirit—one cannot do without the other.

For instance, if one has inspiration only, the mind—being unfruitful—falls into a passive state of idleness. On the other hand, if there is too much information, the mind can be active and enlightened while one's spirit starves from a lack of inspiration. For this reason, there must be a marriage between inspiration and information.

Just because a word is inspirational, doesn't mean that it's informational. There must be a marriage between inspiration and information.

Recently, while attending a conference in Southern California, I was faced with the dilemma between inspiration and information. A friend of mine who was conducting the meetings had arranged for my wife and me to attend some of the evening sessions. On the first night, when it was time for personal ministry, I was summoned onto the platform at the request of my friend and other ministers who were present. I was then told that I would receive encouragement from the Lord.

Since I was desperate for a word from God, I quickly grabbed my wife's hand, moved into position, and expected the best. With my head bowed and my hands lifted high in the air, I assumed the well-known charismatic posture: *Aren't-I-humble?* I was now ready to receive a prophetic word that had the potential to knock my socks off.

At this time a wild-eyed husband and wife team began to circle my wife and me like a Hollywood portrayal of Indians circling a wagon train. After much hoopla, they descended upon us, ready to deliver the word of the Lord. What happened next was no less than a "prophetic scalping." One of them laid his or her hands on my head while the other began a war whoop in unknown tongues. The longer they prayed, the louder they became.

Finally, after a few minutes of rapid-fire tongues, they seemed to run out of ammunition. As a strange quietness filled the room, I took a deep breath and braced myself for the interpretation. Much to my surprise, however, the couple huddled together, conducted a spiritual powwow, and then left the stage. Their attitude seemed to indicate that it was God who had spoken and they were under no obligation to give an interpretation.

I'll never forget the feelings I had that night. I was irritated, frustrated, disillusioned, and totally embarrassed. Most of all, I was disappointed in having received a "word from God" that made absolutely no sense. It was quite an intense and emotional experience, but it failed to bring understanding to my natural mind.

Since then, I have often thought of how the apostle Paul would have reacted in that situation. I have come to the conclusion that this couple would not have escaped without a strong exhortation concerning the proper use of spiritual gifts. I'm certain Paul would have made sure that the next time they attempted to speak for God, they would do it in a way that benefited those receiving the word.

Tongues vs. Prophecy

Two distinct truths emerge simultaneously from First Corinthians 14. We have already identified one as being a warning against excessive use of tongues without an interpretation. The second truth, found in verse 5 of this chapter, is sometimes more difficult for believers to accept because it implies that prophecy has priority over tongues. Paul clearly states:

> *...For greater is he that prophesieth, than he that speaketh with tongues...* (1 Corinthians 14:5).

Upon close examination of this verse, it is evident what it was Paul was saying: The use of the prophetic gift in a church setting is superior to the gift of tongues. The key word used to support this concept is the Greek word *meizon*, which is translated in most English Bibles as "greater." In a broader sense, it also means "larger," or could have been translated as "elder." In any case, the thought could be expressed as this: *He who prophesies has a greater impact on the church than he who speaks with tongues.*

"He that speaketh in an unknown tongue edifieth himself but he that prophesieth edifieth the church" **(1 Corinthians 14:4).**

The reasoning behind Paul's argument in First Corinthians 14:5 is quite obvious. It wasn't a matter of personal preference that motivated him to exalt prophecy over tongues, but rather a desire to see the whole church blessed with a clear word from God. If this could have been done through unknown utterances, then I'm sure he would have had no problem declaring tongues as the greater gift. This doesn't mean that the person who prophesies is greater, but that the gift of prophecy is of greater significance.

Paul's reasoning on this issue is also seen in another Scripture where he declares, "For He that speaketh in an *unknown tongue* speaketh not unto men, but unto God: for no man understandeth him…. But he that prophesieth speaketh unto men to edification, and exhortation, and comfort" (1 Cor. 14:2-3). Paul concludes his thought in First Corinthians 14:4 by writing, "He that speaketh in an *unknown tongue* edifieth himself; but he that prophesieth edifieth the church." Consequently, the real issue is the use of tongues for self-edification, versus edification of the whole church through prophecy. In this context, prophecy becomes the greater gift.

(Note: There is a definite distinction made between the unknown tongue and the gift of tongues. Although the unknown tongue is a personal prayer language spoken in unintelligible form, with no apparent interpretation, the gift of tongues is the ability to utter known languages with the expectation that an interpretation will follow. This is why Paul discourages the use of unknown tongues with no interpretation in a public setting—and encourages prophecy and the gift of tongues, which is accompanied with an interpretation, in a church meeting.)

Making the Transition

Scripture teaches that it is always more blessed to give than to receive. I theorize that these words were in the back of Paul's mind when he instructed the Corinthians on tongues and prophecy. The proof is seen in the way he attempted to divide believers into two categories: tongue-talkers who were content to encourage themselves and those who unselfishly prophesied as a blessing to others. Most Spirit-filled Christians, then and now, fall into one of these categories.

I first learned this distinction many years ago as a young preacher. It all began in the early 1970s when I first launched my ministry as a staff pastor in a charismatic church. I couldn't preach or pastor very well, but I had two other things going for me: I was accomplished in tongue-talking, and I possessed the "knock-em-down anointing."

(For those who may not understand the expression, "knock-em-down anointing," the phrase was first used in the 1970s to describe a phenomenon where people were slain in the Spirit [rendered unconscious] by the laying on of hands. I'm not sure of the connection between speaking in tongues and being slain in the Spirit, but the one seemed to enhance the other. Whatever the association, God often used me to accomplish both.)

In spite of God's anointing upon me, I rarely pastored my church in the traditional sense. I hardly ever visited the newcomers, counseled with the sheep, kissed their babies, married the young couples, or buried the dead. Instead, I just gave myself to the ecstasy of praying in unknown utterances. Of course, I deeply loved the flock, but their midweek crises seemed to distract me from what I considered to be my first calling: praying in tongues.

My reasoning was simple but selfish: Without an overindulgence in tongues (which I desperately needed to strengthen myself), I would never make it as a believer, much less as a minister. My concern was not to fix every little problem in the church, but to build myself up in the most holy faith by praying in tongues. I thought, *And why should this not be a priority? Come Sunday morning there were people waiting to fall down. If I didn't pray in tongues, many of them would be left standing as a testimony to my lack of anointing.* With this mentality, I often forced myself into countless hours of private tongue-talking.

In most instances, after reaching a high plateau of spiritual ecstasy in prayer, I would arise like an Old West gunslinger ready to do battle. I would mount my old Ford Pinto and, with Bible in hand, ride into the sunset looming over our Sunday night service.

When I arrived at the church, I didn't even say, "hello," to the boys who were hanging around the corral. I just dismounted my car and, like a spiritual John Wayne, burst through the church doors with both guns drawn.

Occasionally, without even preaching, I would begin to line the church people up in a row as though they were ducks in a shooting gallery. Big, small, young, or old—it didn't matter to me; none could escape the anointing that blazed out of my spiritual trigger finger. One by one, I would move down the line of people as I spoke in tongues and knocked them down on the floor. Finally, when I had emptied all my spiritual guns, I would holster my smoking fingers and ride out of town without saying another word. If anybody wanted to find me, I would be hiding in my prayer closet, reloading for the next big shoot-out.

It was during one of these prayer times that the Lord began to speak to me about my methods of ministry. One night while praying in tongues, I was interrupted by a voice that said, "Son, what are you doing?" Although I knew this was the Lord speaking to me, I was unsettled by the nature of the question.

I remember thinking: *If God doesn't know what I am doing, then I must really be in trouble!* I replied to God, "Lord, I'm doing what Your Word says: speaking in tongues."

At this point, He asked me a second question that was even more unsettling than the first. He said, "Son, do you know what you are praying about?"

Again, my answer was scriptural as I replied, "Lord, my understanding is unfruitful, but my spirit knows exactly what I'm saying." That was the last time I got a chance to respond in the conversation!

In a loving way, God began to explain to me the finer points of mature ministry. He indicated that I had been using His anointing primarily to put people to sleep; whereas, His desire was to awaken them to the truth. He said, "*Knocking people unconscious on the floor is fine, but the greater need is to resurrect the saints so they might hear what the Spirit is saying to the Church.*" He continued to instruct me in this matter, urging me to use my native tongue when ministering to the people. I would be allowed to continue knocking them down, He implied, but I must also give them an intelligible word from the Lord.

At that time I wasn't able to fully understand the implications of my little talk with God. Even so, I did begin to make a transition from tongues to prophecy. The next Sunday when people came forward to be slain in the Spirit, I refrained from speaking to them in tongues. It was hard to change my model of ministry; nevertheless, I operated in the greater gift by speaking simple words of prophecy over two or three people.

I'm not convinced that my words had much of an impact on anyone that day. However, I am certain that I made the proper adjustment in the administration of my ministry. From that day forward, I gained greater understanding of the significant role that prophecy plays within the Church. Most importantly, this experience created a desire within me to encourage others to exercise the gift of prophecy as well as the gift of tongues.

In spite of this newfound zeal, my ability to lead people into the prophetic was soon stifled by questions relating to who can prophesy. I was often asked, "Is prophetic expression exclusively relegated to mature believers among the male leadership? Can women and children prophesy? And, if so, how do we nurture and raise up the prophetic within the Body of Christ?" These are some of the issues we shall explore in the next chapter.

Chapter Five

WHO can prophesy?

In today's Church, people are asking serious questions about the ownership of prophecy. Is the whole Church called to the prophetic? Do sheep have the same privileges as shepherds? What is the role of women in prophetic ministry? Can children speak prophetically? These are some of the issues that transcend cultural and ecclesiastical barriers and create a controversy within the entire Body of Christ.

In recent years, I have witnessed more quarrels and hurt feelings over the issue of who can prophesy than any other issue pertaining to the prophetic. This conflict has defiled the hearts of some of our best pastors and has provided an opportunity for many in the church to develop attitude problems that border upon sheer rebellion. Forbidden to prophesy, these sheep stray from their sheepfolds in search of greener prophetic pastures.

In most cases, whether male or female, the opinion of bruised prophetic sheep is unanimous. They sincerely believe that most leaders are overcontrolling and heavy-handed with prophetic people. Although this behavior is not true of all ministers, the fears of these sheep seem to be heightened by the attitudes of a few pastors and elders who are opposed to any kind of prophetic flow within their churches. Especially damaging are those leaders who deny the right of exercising the gift of prophecy to anyone but themselves.

Do church leaders who attempt to corner the market on prophecy have a scriptural basis for their actions? Of course not! Paul indicates in his letters to the Corinthians that all may prophesy. He also encourages all believers in First Corinthians 14:1 to desire spiritual gifts, especially prophecy.

In spite of Paul's exhortation, however, many of these leaders today believe they are called to protect the Church from the weirdness that often surrounds the prophetic. They are absolutely convinced that the gift of prophecy is dangerous in the hands of undeveloped sheep. As a result, only the designated *mature ones*, such as elders and associate pastors, can prophesy in their church. All others must sit in silence, hoping for the day that their leaders determine they are mature enough to be released in their gifting.

In most instances, this sort of unwritten theology seems to dominate the realm of ecclesiastical thinking. As indicated, the underlying logic may seem reasonable, but the outcome is counterproductive to prophetic growth in the Church. Therefore, the apostle Paul instructs us in First Corinthians 14:31 to prophesy "one by one, that all may learn." Apparently, his emphasis wasn't on the theological perfection of prophecy, but on training those who are developing the use of their prophetic gift.

Basic prophetic ministry such as edification, exhortation, and comfort belong to all who have a heart to build up the Body of Christ.

Does this mean that we are to ignore other scriptural guidelines for prophecy? Absolutely not! I readily agree with those who are committed to theological and spiritual purity that there is a tremendous need to handle the prophetic with reverence and godly wisdom. By no means should we allow those who are immature to deliberately bring a reproach upon the name of the Lord, nor should beginners bear the responsibility for giving prophetic words of correction or direction. Yet, we must also remember that basic prophetic ministry such as edification, exhortation, and comfort belong to all who have a heart to build up the Body of Christ.

> *But there remained two of the men in the camp, the name of the one was Eldad, and the name of the other Medad...and they prophesied in the camp. And there ran a young man, and told Moses, and said, Eldad and Medad do prophesy in the camp. And Joshua the son of Nun, the servant of Moses, one of his young men, answered and said, My lord Moses, forbid them. And Moses said unto him, Enviest thou for my sake?* **would God that all the Lord's people were prophets, and that the Lord would put His spirit upon them!** (Numbers 11:26-29)

Maturity vs. Availability

Determining who can flow in the prophetic does not always revolve around maturity or eldership, but around availability. In many instances in the New Testament, it was often the common folk and new converts who prophesied under the inspiration of the Holy Spirit. They prophesied not because they were schooled, experienced, or mature in prophecy, but because they were available.

The apostle Paul understood this principle of availabilty and instructed the Corinthian church that "all prophesy" (see 1 Cor. 14:31). His exhortation to prophesy was not directed to a handful of mature leaders, but to all who were open and accessible. In the Book of Acts he demonstrated this truth by laying hands on common believers and imparting the Holy Spirit to them. As a result, they also prophesied.

 Determining who can flow in the prophetic does not always revolve around maturity or eldership, but around availability.

This dynamic is also illustrated in other instances in the Bible. For example, in the Old Testament, availability seemed to characterize the life and ministry of Moses and his older brother, Aaron. Initially, God appeared to Moses at a burning bush and appointed him as a prophet/deliverer to Israel. Yet, Moses felt incapable of fulfilling this great commission by himself and petitioned the Lord for a helper. Therefore, Aaron, his brother, came under the umbrella of Moses' calling and took command of the prophetic office. Aaron became God's spokesman, not because he was tremendously talented or even experienced, but because he was available. As a result, Moses and Aaron labored together as one of the first prophetic teams.

In the Book of Numbers, we see further indications that prophetic anointing was given to other men who yielded themselves to the Spirit of God. In addition to Aaron, 70 elders also received a prophetic mantle. It is recorded in Numbers 11:25 that "the Lord came down in a cloud, and spake unto him [Moses], and took of the spirit that was upon him [Moses], and gave it unto the seventy elders: and it came to pass, that, when the spirit rested upon them, they prophesied, and did not cease."

Again, in my opinion, these 70 elders received prophetic impartation not because they were special, but because they were open to receiving a word from God. They were in the right place at the right time and displayed a willingness to accommodate their leader. Consequently, they not only prophesied, but also appeared to operate under Moses' mantle of authority for the rest of their lives.

Like Aaron and the 70 elders, we, too, must be available to the ministry of the Holy Spirit. We must not be as concerned with *who* can prophesy, as we are with *when* and *where* we can prophesy. We must understand that in God's Kingdom both sheep and shepherd, mature and immature, educated and uneducated, are released to flow in prophetic utterance.

Women in Ministry

We shall now turn our attention to one of the more volatile issues of the Church today: the role of women in ministry. Does the Bible encourage women to prophesy? Do they have authority to address a church prophetically? Can they hold prophetic office? Before I address these questions, I would like to note that much of my thinking presented in the next few pages was inspired by reading *The Apostle Paul and Women in the Church* by Dr. Don Williams (published by Regal Books, 1977).

According to Dr. Williams, some believe the writings of the apostle Paul prohibit women from participating in spiritual ministry—other than an occasional utterance of prophecy. Others are of the opinion that Paul had a heart to affirm women in ministry, but was hindered by the culture and traditions of his day. Yet, how can the Bible be the infallible Word of God if one assumes that its writers leaned toward ancient custom? Where do we draw the line between eternal truth and cultural truth? Were the writers of the Bible merely responding to the needs of their generation? And, if men of God, like the apostle Paul, are wrong about women's roles, how can we trust the rest of their writings?

The conflict over a *woman's place* is nothing new to the Church. It almost seems as if the apostle Paul, himself, was unclear on this issue. At times, Paul seemed to be adamant, demanding women to be veiled, silent, and subordinate to men. Yet, in Galatians 3:28, he sets women free by declaring, "There is neither...male nor female...in Christ Jesus." Paul never allowed a woman to be ordained, but quite often he spoke affectionately of women who were co-laborers in the gospel.

These contrasting positions are painfully frustrating for women and men alike. As a result of this paradox, the attitude of today's Church toward women in ministry swings from one end of the pendulum to the other. So extreme are the opinions of some, that a literal war of words has developed between the two sides. The one side strongly demands equality for women in the Church, while the other dogmatically denies the ministerial office to any female. With these kinds of extremes, it is no wonder that the world views the Church as confused and double-minded.

In spite of seeming contradictions, I believe that Paul's writings were birthed by the inspiration of the Holy Spirit, even those

Scriptures we consider to be hard to understand. Although much of his writing reflects historical situations that must be interpreted in context, it also is apparent that Paul is consistent in his understanding of the role of women in the Church. As a proven apostle and theologian, he lays out a delicate balance of Scripture that is often misinterpreted as being too complex for the average believer. Even so, when all of Paul's writings are viewed in context, a simple thread of truth emerges!

First, Paul was not a woman-hater as some may think. In fact, he commends a number of women in his epistles. According to Dr. Williams, in the Book of Romans, Paul sends affectionate greetings to more than half a dozen women of God. This list includes: *Phoebe*, the deaconess; *Priscilla*, a fellow worker in Christ; *Mary*, who labored among the church; *Tryphaena* and *Tryphosa*, sisters who were workers in the Lord; the *mother of Rufus*, who was a mother also to Paul; *Julia*, a Roman female; and the *sister of Nereus*, who was counted among the saints. Paul clearly displays a fondness for women—a fondness unsurpassed by the other apostles.

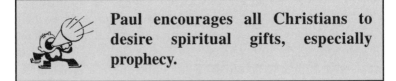

Paul encourages all Christians to desire spiritual gifts, especially prophecy.

Next, Paul encourages *all* Christians to desire spiritual gifts, especially prophecy. In light of this exhortation, it's apparent that, in the realm of the gifts of the Spirit, there are no restraints on women as some suppose. It's true that Paul instructs the Corinthian women to keep silent in the church, but, as indicated, we must understand the historic implications of this statement.

In the Corinthian church, women and children were seated on one side; men were seated on the other side. Due to this seating arrangement, it is believed that the wives could not hear what was being said. As a result, the women interrupted the meetings by yelling questions to their husbands who were seated across the room. In response to this confusion, Paul had no choice but to restrict the voice of the Corinthian women. Paul's command to keep silent was not a spiritual issue but an issue of culture and order. It was never intended to be taken out of the context of his day or arbitrarily applied to diverse cultures. Nor was it to be used to devalue women in the Church, then or now. Had Paul known that such abuse would occur, I'm sure he would have defined his intentions more clearly.

Function vs. Office

Many believe that Paul draws a clear theological line between ministry function and office. Those who hold this view readily agree that women can operate in the gifts of the Spirit and flow in spiritual ministry. Yet, they deny females access to the governmental offices of apostle, prophet, evangelist, pastor, and teacher listed in Ephesians 4:11.

Their reasoning is twofold. To begin, they hold to the theology of male headship found in many Old and New Testament writings. The idea is that men alone are given leadership roles in both family and Church government. Paul seems to promote this concept as divine order by declaring, "...the head of every man is Christ; and the head of the woman is the man..." (1 Cor. 11:3).

He further strengthens this chain of authority, which is God-Christ-Men-Women-Children, by prohibiting those who are under authority from usurping the authority of those over them. In this instance, it is the woman who is forbidden "to teach, nor to usurp authority over the man" (1 Tim. 2:12). Therefore, in regard to these Scriptures, many believe that women can freely minister under the leadership of men, but cannot lead or rule in a governmental position within the Church, especially a position of apostle or prophet.

Another argument that many use to exclude women from functioning in the five offices is that God gave governmental "gifts unto *men,*" not women. In Ephesians 4, Paul speaks of Christ's distributing the ministry offices to the Church, and writes, "...He [Jesus] led captivity captive, and gave gifts unto men. ... And He gave some, apostles; and some, prophets; and some, evangelists; and some, pastors and teachers" (Eph. 4:8,11). Many teach that had these offices been given to both sexes, Paul would have used, "men and women" in this verse instead of signifying the male as the beneficiary of the fivefold ministry.

I personally disagree with this sort of reasoning and feel it is wrong to exclude women from the ministry offices of Ephesians 4, especially from the office of prophetess. It's true that the Creator established a divine order for the role of men and women. However, we must also consider that some of Paul's writings were influenced by ancient custom and culture, and the historical setting in which he lived was filled with bias against women. For that reason, in fairness to those who affirm women in ministry, we will focus more specifically on a believer in the New Testament named *Junias.*

Junias

Both in the Old and the New Testaments we see women who seem to be in conflict with the Pauline writings. Deborah, who was called a "prophetess" in the Old Testament, ruled over Israel as a judge and also led its army into battle. Sarah, who is considered to be a perfect model of submission, challenged the authority of her mate more than once. In one instance, God commanded Abraham to obey Sarah's voice—as if it were the word of the Lord—and cast out his concubine and her son Ishmael (see Gen. 21:9-12).

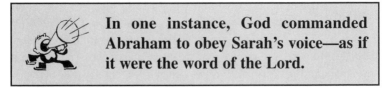

In one instance, God commanded Abraham to obey Sarah's voice—as if it were the word of the Lord.

In the writings of the New Testament, we see further evidence of women with spiritual authority. In the Book of Luke there was Anna, the prophetess who served God both night and day in the Temple. As already mentioned, Phoebe was a faithful deaconess to the church at Cenchrea. Philip the evangelist had four daughters who were noted for their prophetic gifting.

Scores of other women could also be added to the long list of those who ministered in the early Church. More specifically, evidence exists that possibly links the New Testament believer named *Junias* to the office of apostle. Paul writes in Romans 16:7 (RSV), "Greet Andronicus and *Junias*, my kinsmen and my fellow prisoners; they are men of note among the apostles, and they were in Christ before me."

In the book *The Apostle Paul and Women in the Church* (pages 44-45), Dr. Don Williams approaches Junias in this manner:

> "The unresolved issue is whether *Junias* in Greek is a masculine contraction of *Junianus* or the feminine of Junia. The spelling in the original language is the same for either possibility. Furthermore, the phrase 'they are men of note' literally reads they are of note. 'Men' is absent in the Greek, and is inserted by the translators. Thus, Paul could be referring to a woman here, quite probably a husband-wife team....This would mean that Junia is a kinsman, that is, a Jew. She is also a fellow prisoner, that is she, like Paul, had suffered incarceration for her faith in Christ. Most surprising, Junia is also an apostle, an early convert even before Paul. This has lead most commentators to render the proper name as the masculine Junias rather than Junia. While a final decision cannot be reached from the text, why must we suppose that no woman could be called an apostle by Paul?

> "Only the extra-Biblical assumption that a woman could not be an apostle keeps most commentators from reading Junias as Junia. The church father Chrysostom had no such bias. He writes, 'and indeed to be apostles at all is a great thing. But to be even amongst these of note, just consider what a great encomium this is! But they were of note owing to their works, to their achievements.' *Oh! How great is the devotion of this woman, that she should be even counted worthy of the appellation of this apostle!*"

Call for Balance

It is obvious that Scripture can be interpreted in such a way as to support either side of the debate on women. I must confess that I have drifted between the extremes of these two opinions. However, I am convinced of three things that I consider to be absolutely clear and non-negotiable.

First, women can prophesy, preach, teach, heal, and evangelize. This is not to say, however, that there are no restrictions placed on either gender when it comes to expressing the different gifts of God. Remember, preaching and teaching the Bible are not necessarily the same as functioning in the office of a teacher. Likewise, the ability to prophesy is not always an indication that we are called to the office of a prophet.

Second, I am convinced that as a male-dominated, cold Church, we desperately need to receive input from our women. The warmth, spiritual sensitivity, and nurturing instincts of women are invaluable to the family of God. As indicated, the Bible resonates with numerous examples of women who greatly contributed to the welfare of the Church.

Finally, both Simeon (male) and Anna (female) prophesied over the baby Jesus in the Book of Luke. In my opinion, it will also take the combined efforts of today's men and women to prophetically bring forth Christ in the end-time Church. This is a divine pattern that must be embraced by all who believe that God "will pour out My spirit upon all flesh; and your sons and your daughters shall prophesy..." (Joel 2:28).

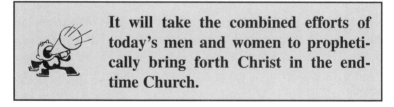

It will take the combined efforts of today's men and women to prophetically bring forth Christ in the end-time Church.

Children and Prophecy

In light of the prophet Joel's exhortation, it's obvious that men and women have the privilege to prophesy. Yet, can our children also prophesy? And more importantly, can we trust these prophecies? To begin with, God is certainly not above speaking to us through the agency of a child. Since He has encouraged us to have the faith of little children (see Mk. 10:15), it is not unreasonable to expect that God could or would use small children to accurately communicate with His adult children.

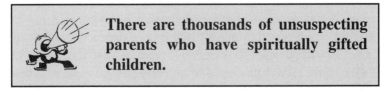

There are thousands of unsuspecting parents who have spiritually gifted children.

In view of this fact, I believe there are thousands of unsuspecting parents who have spiritually gifted children. I entreat these parents to cultivate a sensitivity to the Spirit of God within their children. The spiritual potential that lies within their souls may one day surprise you and could easily serve to protect you! Their strange dreams and childlike impressions may seem insignificant at first; but in many instances, these children are prophetic in nature. If the gift that lies within them is nurtured, God might eventually commission a prophet from within your own family.

What truth do we have to support the truth that God would use the innocence, the meekness, and the trusting nature of our children to establish a prophetic platform for this generation? It's apparent in the Bible that God is raising up a prophetic generation, beginning with the least among us! The apostle Peter declared this truth in Acts 2:17. Quoting the prophet Joel, Peter said, "And it shall come to pass in the last days, saith God, I will pour out of My Spirit upon all flesh: and your *sons* and your *daughters* shall prophesy...."

There are two things in this portion of Scripture to support the claim that God speaks through prophetic children today. First, Peter indicates that a great outpouring of prophetic anointing would be unleashed in the last days. Of course, we who are alive today make up a large part of this last day's generation. Also, Peter made it very clear that our sons and daughters today would engage in both receiving and speaking prophetic utterances. This is especially true of children who are encouraged to "desire prophetic ministry."

Is there further biblical proof that supports the concept of prophetic children? Yes! Although Peter's exhortation was directed toward a *coming generation*, there were a number of prophetic children who lived in ancient Israel. Consider for a moment the life of an Old Testament boy named Samuel. In First Samuel 3:1-18 (NKJ), God visited this child at an early age and spoke to him concerning his master Eli:

> *Then the boy Samuel ministered to the Lord before Eli...and while Samuel was lying down...the Lord called Samuel. And he answered, "Here I am"...Now the Lord came and stood and called as at other times, "Samuel! Samuel!" And Samuel answered, "Speak, for Your servant hears."...Then Eli called Samuel and said..."What is the word that the Lord spoke to you?..." Then Samuel told him everything....*

The Bible provides us with several other examples much like Samuel's encounter with the prophetic. We could discuss the God-given dreams of a boy named Joseph or the adventures of a young Saul who found his lost donkeys by heeding a prophetic word. However, in keeping with our focus upon prophetic children today, I feel it's important to examine some more recent examples, which illustrate that prophetic revelation is not limited to the lives of biblical characters, but is also common among children today.

Prophetic revelation is not limited to the lives of biblical characters, but is also common among children today.

Prophetic Daughters

Recently, I had a conversation with a friend about the prophetic tendencies of one of his daughters. Her name is Christa. Her father, Timothy, explained that Christa seems to have prior knowledge about things unknowable at the time. In some instances, she has accurately forecast the time, place, and Richter scale readings of earthquakes. This began some years ago when she dreamed about a major quake that hit California.

Now, it doesn't take a prophet to predict earthquakes in California, but it is difficult to pinpoint the exact time and Richter scale reading. Christa did both. Within a few days of her dream, we encountered one of the strongest quakes to hit the West Coast in recent years.

If Christa's prediction was only one isolated incident, I would be inclined to dismiss her premonitions. Yet, the truth is that many of her prophetic impressions have come to pass. Recently she had another vision about a major earthquake in this nation— an earthquake registering extremely high on the Richter scale. I am inclined to believe Christa, not because she is a friend of the family, but because she is a highly prophetic child.

Prophetic Sons

In my estimation Christa is just one of the thousands of children to whom God is speaking today. I also believe that the prophetic words of Christa and others like her have greater significance than we have ever realized. In fact, there are those who believe these children possess revelatory information that is directly related to such things as current world affairs, catastrophic weather changes, personal warnings, etc. I, too, am convinced that this is true.

For instance, Roland, one of my own children, had an amazing encounter with prophetic perception. He awoke one morning with a foreboding sense that something bad was going to happen that day. He cried for a long time, begging his mother not to send him to school. Knowing that Roland loved school, my wife, Rebecca, became concerned about the source of his apprehension. All he would say was, "Please don't make me go, Mom. I just feel something is wrong!"

In spite of his great reluctance to leave the house, Roland was put on the school bus by a very puzzled mother, who thought: *Was there a possibility that Roland was perceiving imminent danger? Did he really hear from God?* Her head told her, "no," but her heart said to pray for the welfare of her child. So, for a period of time she gave herself to tearful intercession.

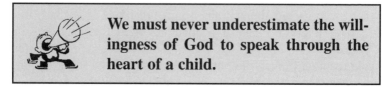

We must never underestimate the willingness of God to speak through the heart of a child.

Within an hour, the bus, now fully loaded with children, overturned on a remote bridge and fell into raging floodwaters. The situation was more than critical. The waters were swift and deep; the bus was beginning to sink. To further complicate matters, no one was near to hear the frantic pleas for help. It seemed that all would be lost.

Then, just in the nick of time, one of the kids managed to jump from the bus and swim to the edge of the river. Screaming for help, he ran to a nearby house. As a result, a call was made to the proper authorities, who immediately dispatched a rescue unit to the scene of the accident. Due to the heroic efforts of the rescue team, none of the children suffered major injury. One by one, they were pulled to safety as the bus slowly drifted downstream. When all the children were finally on the riverbank, the bus abruptly shifted position and sank into the depths of the swirling waters.

Although credit was given to the people involved in the rescue, we believe that the safety of those children was ensured earlier that morning. Had it not been for the prophetic warning that prompted my wife to fervent prayer, we believe that Roland and the other children would have been severely hurt or even killed. Several of the families involved in that community—upon hearing about Roland's foreboding sense and knowing Rebecca and the value she placed upon prayer and intercession—attributed this to a miraculous intervention by God. The local newspaper reported the no-fatality accident as nothing less than a miracle.

This event, and others like it, accentuate my heartfelt belief that we must never underestimate the willingness of God to speak through the heart of a child. Jesus said that "out of the mouth of babes and sucklings Thou hast perfected praise" (Mt. 21:16). The prophet Isaiah underscores this thought by declaring that "a little child shall lead them" (Is. 11:6). I am aware of the broader interpretation concerning these two passages of Scripture, but the aforementioned application is also true. *Children today can have spiritual gifts, especially the gift of prophecy.*

Nurturing the Prophetic in Our Children

How do we begin to develop the prophetic gifts that are resident within our children? The answer is fourfold. First, Scripture charges us to "bring them up [our children] in the nurture and admonition of the Lord" (Eph. 6:4). Second, our lives could someday depend on a word from a prophetic child. Third, Exodus 19:6 informs us that God has called them to be a kingdom of priests to our succeeding generations. Finally, as previously indicated, Jesus declared, "out of the mouth of babes and sucklings Thou hast perfected praise" (Mt. 21:16).

If we believe these things are true, then what methods must we employ to nurture the prophetic within our children?

1. Teach your children that God wishes to speak to them, even as children.
2. Read Scriptures to your children and tell them Bible stories pertaining to the prophetic.
3. Lay hands on your children daily, if possible, praying for the prophetic gift to be stirred within them.
4. Speak prophetically to your child's spirit, prophesying God's intent for him or her (see Joel 2:28).
5. Encourage your children to share even their simplest dreams or impressions with you.
6. Teach your children to interpret their dreams in the context of Scripture and with its symbolic implications.

7. When possible, expose your children to valid prophetic ministry.

Exposing our children to valid prophetic ministry cannot be overemphasized. In many instances, their prophetic gift is received and fostered through impartation, as opposed to systematic, in-depth teaching of Scripture. Although sound biblical instruction is vital, we must remember that *more is caught than taught*. Therefore, to fulfill God's mandate to raise up a prophetic generation in the fear and admonition of the Lord, we must not only teach them about the prophetic, but also model it in front of them.

Conclusion

Whether church leader or laity, male or female, child or adult, it is imperative for Christians to understand the basic role that prophecy plays within their own lives and the life of the Church. When God elected to pour out His Spirit upon all flesh, He had a definite prophetic purpose in mind. As prophetic people, we must align ourselves with this purpose.

In Part Two of this book, we will discuss the purpose of prophecy, and also examine how the prophetic is designed to bring edification, exhortation, comfort, conviction, direction, and forthtelling to the Body of Christ.

Part Two

Explaining the Purpose and Place of Prophecy in the Church

Chapter Six

Basic prophetic

To possess a gift without purpose is to waste the gift that has been given. The same can be true of prophetic ministry. It is one thing to receive a prophetic anointing and yet another to have prophetic purpose. Just as a river needs earthen banks to direct its flow, the prophetic needs specific guidelines to channel its awesome force.

Those who are maturing as prophets can easily identify with this principle of focus and purpose. As a prophetic ministry is initially developed, there is a season when it is seems sufficient to *just prophesy*. In the mind of an aspiring or undeveloped prophet, the actual act of speaking a prophetic word often takes precedence over the clarity or scriptural importance of that word.

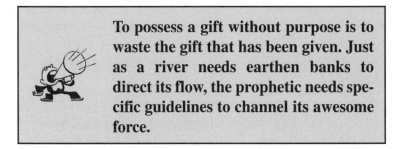

To possess a gift without purpose is to waste the gift that has been given. Just as a river needs earthen banks to direct its flow, the prophetic needs specific guidelines to channel its awesome force.

Nonetheless, when the novelty of the prophetic eventually wears thin, most Christians are left with a deep conviction that *without a purpose the people perish*. In time, the thrill of aimless prophecy gives way to the desire to be an accurate dispenser of God's truth. As a result, the prophet learns to minister in a focused, concise, and specific flow of prophetic utterance.

In my own experience with prophetic ministry, I, too, have dealt with this issue of purpose. As previously stated, I was happy to make the transition from tongues to prophecy in the early days of my ministry. However, shortly afterward I became content to utter poetic prophecies within the confines of our Sunday church services. I was not always sure of what I said or how it applied to the listeners, but for the most part I was happy just to release my gift. Like a runaway train off its tracks, I would charge into the meetings with every ounce of prophetic strength I had. There was hardly a Sunday I didn't toot my horn and blow tons of prophetic smoke.

Eventually, it seemed that God and His people had enough of me and my gift. I was asked to cool my spiritual engines and pray for wisdom. Although I was offended, my heart bore witness to the notion that I should pull back on the throttle for a while. After slowing down a bit and evaluating the effectiveness of my ministry, I soon realized my weakness. My prophecies were lacking in purpose and direction.

In an attempt to correct this lack of prophetic focus, I, along with many others, began to establish definite guidelines for prophesying. The goal was clear. We were determined to bring wild, unfocused prophecies under control. Aimless utterances that generated more confusion than revelation were put to rest, no matter how poetic or spiritual they appeared to be. From that time forward, we began to focus more on the purpose of each prophecy rather than on its profundity.

Aimless utterances that generate more confusion than revelation need to be put to rest, no matter how poetic or spiritual they appear to be.

At first, the guidelines we installed were simple. The rules were:

a. Avoid utterances that are mystical and are not direct and down-to-earth.
b. Don't prophesy contrary to the spiritual flow of a service or interrupt those who are teaching the Word.
c. Avoid prophesying to women unless their husbands are present.
d. Never embarrass people by divulging secret sins—publicly.
e. Refrain from giving directive words in a private setting.
f. When possible, do not use the gift of prophecy to discourage the Church.

For a while, this prophetic protocol was sufficient; but as the Body of Christ began to grow, things became more complex. Therefore, in an attempt to further refine prophetic ministry, we added more specific guidelines to the list. Some of these included:

g. Never rebuke an elder through prophecy.
h. Stay away from prophetic matchmaking, especially prophesying marriages.
i. Always use caution when predicting the birth of babies.
j. Avoid the temptation to prophesy wealth and riches to young sheep.
k. Never show partiality when delivering the word of the Lord.

Installing these safeguards seemed to be the right thing to do at the time. If nothing else, they brought a certain credibility to our crude beginnings. Yet, in spite of our willingness to be accountable, our focus seemed to be on *what not to do*, as opposed to *what to do*. We were negative in our approach rather than positive. Our attempt to give structure and purpose to the

 If prophecy is a biblical gift, then the blueprint for its operation is also found in the Bible.

prophetic was noble, but not always scriptural. The result was confusion and debate.

Many years have passed since those early days of my prophetic ministry. However, the questions remain the same. What is the antidote for random and unfocused prophecies? How can we bring clarity and meaning to prophetic ministry? Can we use our gift to further the purpose of God in the earth and minister effectively to the Body of Christ? If so, then how do we accomplish these things?

The answers to these questions are not as vague as some might think. If prophecy is a biblical gift, then the blueprint for its operation is also found in the Bible. More specifically, these issues are clearly addressed in the New Testament, especially in Paul's letter to the Corinthian church. Therefore, in the following sections of this chapter I will examine some of the more crucial purposes of prophecy as detailed in Scripture and highlight them with personal experience.

Edification

> *But he that prophesieth speaketh unto men to **edification**, and exhortation, and comfort* (1 Corinthians 14:3).

Throughout the history of the Church, many believers have been sustained through the power of prophetic edification. In both the Old and New Testaments, we find men of God who were built up in their faith and motivated to press forward as a result of prophetic encouragement. Included in this list of benefactors was a weary king named David, a religious zealot named Saul (who later became the apostle Paul), a young pastor of the early Church named Timothy, and our Lord Jesus Himself (see 1 Chron. 17:7-15; Acts 9:10-18; 1 Tim. 1:18; Lk. 2:27-33). All of these men were strengthened and empowered by God through prophetic words of edification.

Although various other accounts of prophetic edification are found in the Bible, prophetic words of encouragement are not simply relegated to the historical Church. We desperately need this encouragement in today's world of demonic oppression and social stress. Paul instructs us to "keep encouraging one another so that none of you is hardened by the lure of sin" (Heb. 3:13 JB). Also, in First Thessalonians 5:11, the apostle admonishes Christians to "comfort yourselves together, and edify one another." In First Corinthians 14:12, he writes, "...strive to excel in building up the church" (RSV). In Ephesians 4:16, he introduces the thought that the Body of Christ is built up and encouraged "unto the edifying of itself in love."

In light of Paul's writings, we, as Christians, have no other option than to dispense encouragement and edification to the Body of Christ. Yet, before we are proficient in this ministry, we must understand the full biblical concept of edification.

For instance, the Greek word *oikadome* is often translated as "edification." It is also rendered "building." Thus, the words *edification* and *building* are interchangeable throughout much of the New Testament. Overall, these two words actually mean "to build up, construct, confirm, establish, and improve."

When the Jews referred to the building of the Temple in John 2:20, *oikadome* is used. Likewise, the term *oikadome* is also applied to believers who "as living stones, are being *built up* [*oikadome*] a spiritual house" (1 Pet. 2:5 NKJ). In one instance, edification denotes the construction of a natural temple. Elsewhere, it clearly indicates the building up of the saints of God. Therefore, in light of the need to build up the Body of Christ, Christians who are determined to operate in the prophetic should concentrate on using their gifts to facilitate the ministry of edification.

The need for building up the Body through edification and encouragement was made very clear to me at the beginning of my ministry. While I was meditating upon the priorities of the prophetic, God began to speak to me in a most unusual fashion. In a near-audible voice that seemed to penetrate my entire being, He said:

"One of the greatest ministries you can ever possess is the ministry of encouragement. In a world without hope,

people need the affirmation of My love. Signs, wonders, miracles, healing, and teaching are important, but are secondary to the great commission of encouragement."

He continued to say:

*"Encouragement is the motivational force behind the ministry of Jesus and should also be the priority of all Christians. So, bless rather than curse, **build up where others have torn down, and always use your gift for the edification of mankind.**"*

Many years have passed since God spoke to me; however, this simple word is indelibly imprinted on my heart. As a result, I have learned to resist the temptation to unnecessarily reprove the Church. By choosing to prophesy positive words of edification, I've seen the joy of life restored to suicidal people. I've seen insanely depressed people completely delivered from their torment. Weary Christians on the brink of despair have been encouraged to try again. Broken marriages have been mended, and rebellious children have turned to the Lord. All this happens because a word fitly spoken accomplishes much more than a rebuke out of season.

So, for those prophetic people who feel compelled to bludgeon the Body of Christ with their gift, I have a few things to say. To begin, we must first develop a deep conviction that God is *not* angry with His people. He loves them unconditionally and wants His prophets to speak to them in a kind manner. There may be occasions when it is necessary to prophesy correction and rebuke, but these should come as a last resort, not as a first response.

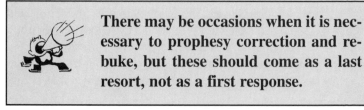

There may be occasions when it is necessary to prophesy correction and rebuke, but these should come as a last resort, not as a first response.

Next, when relating to God's Church, we are called to be Body-builders, not wife-beaters. Be forewarned: When the Chief

Shepherd returns, we will give an account for the stewardship of the gifts He has given us to encourage and build up His Bride. Consequently, if we are abusive to the Lord's wife, we must prepare ourselves for the judgment of God against those who, in spite of their commission to edify the Church, habitually malign her.

Finally, we will be judged for every harmful word that proceeds out of our mouths. In which case, we should not let "evil talk come out of [our] mouths, but only such as is good for edifying, as fits the occasion, that it may impart grace to those who hear" (Eph. 4:29 RSV). Jesus said, "Truly, I say to you, as you did it to one of the least of these My brethren, you did it to Me" (Mt. 25:40 RSV).

Exhortation

*But he that prophesieth speaketh unto men to edification, and **exhortation**, and comfort* (1 Corinthians 14:3).

The word *exhortation* is closely associated with the word *edification*. Both of these words denote encouragement. Though similar, there is enough difference between the two to justify an investigation into the more specific meaning of exhortation.

Webster's Dictionary defines exhortation in this manner: "To urge or incite by strong argument, advice or appeal; to admonish earnestly." This definition is quite distinct from the *building up* of edification. *Strong's Concordance* verifies this distinction by rendering exhortation as "The act of crying out, wooing and calling near." Thus, the word *exhortation*, as related to prophetic utterance, means "to prompt and urge the Church to draw near to God."

I am convinced that a major part of prophetic ministry is given to help propel the Church forward in Christ. True prophets do this by first discerning God's intentions for His people, and then they cautiously urge the Church to go forward in that general direction. Paul makes this clear to Timothy in Second Timothy 4:2, where he instructs the young preacher to "exhort with all longsuffering." The image is one of a shepherd who patiently leads his sheep. He doesn't angrily drive the flock but gently urges them on to greener pastures.

In the same way, prophets must gently direct the Church toward Christ. When prophetically addressing the people of God, it is wise for the prophetic person to steer clear of harsh ultimatums. Prophecies that present God as being eternally angry, intolerant, unmerciful, and ready to kill should be avoided at all cost. Fear tactics and excessive pressure have never been the basis of biblical protocol and never will be. God is a God of love who motivates out of love. Satan is the one who uses fear to promote his purpose.

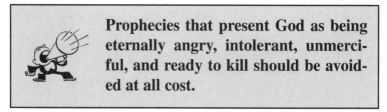

Prophecies that present God as being eternally angry, intolerant, unmerciful, and ready to kill should be avoided at all cost.

For this reason, the Bible sets clear boundaries for exhortation. We are instructed in Scripture to exhort those who are weary to cleave unto the Lord! All who have failed to gird their minds with truth are also exhorted to be sober-minded. Exhortation is also given to prayerless Christians in order that they might give themselves to much prayer and supplication. Most importantly, those who are discouraged are exhorted to continue in the faith. (See Acts 11:23; 14:22; 1 Timothy 2:1; Titus 2:6.)

Don't misunderstand me! I am not promoting a faint-hearted form of prophetic ministry that tolerates the indulgence of gross sin. I am acutely aware that there are times when the Lord calls us to boldly rebuke those who repeatedly resist the wooing of the Holy Spirit. Yet, when leading the flock, we must understand that it is goats who need to be pushed, not sheep.

Comfort

> *But he that prophesieth speaketh unto men to edification, and exhortation, and **comfort*** (1 Corinthians 14:3).

Another fundamental purpose of prophetic ministry is to comfort. This characteristic is often known as consolation. Its root form means "to come alongside." *Comfort* also means "to strengthen and to reinforce." It denotes physical, mental, and spiritual refreshment. In both the Old and New Testaments, comfort stems from the tender love of God for His people. Often, it counterbalances the troubles of life and rescues us from the discouragement encountered in the work of the Lord.

> **A fundamental purpose of prophetic ministry is to comfort.**

To comfort the brokenhearted is a highly valued virtue in the Kingdom of God. This is seen throughout much of the Bible when prophets repeatedly pronounced God's lovingkindness toward His people. "For the Lord shall comfort Zion" (Is. 51:3a). When prophesying the future ministry of Jesus, Isaiah writes, "The spirit of the Lord God is upon Me; because the Lord hath anointed Me...to comfort all that mourn" (Is. 61:1-2).

In the New Testament, we are also told that God is the "God of all comfort" (2 Cor. 1:3). Jesus strengthens this truth by saying, "I will not leave you comfortless" (Jn. 14:18). Years later, the apostle Paul declared that God "comforteth us in all of our tribulation" (2 Cor. 1:4). He continued by exhorting believers to "comfort yourselves together," "comfort the feebleminded," and to "comfort those that are cast down" (see 1 Thess. 5:11,14; 2 Cor. 7:6).

Considering the importance of these Scriptures, it's expedient for prophetic people to speak comfortingly to the people of God. We must realize that judgment spoken through prophecy doesn't always reach the heart of an indifferent Church. Instead, it is the goodness of God that leads us to repentance. This truth is supported by James who declares, "Mercy triumphs against judgment" (Jas. 2:13 NIV; see also Is. 40:2; Rom. 2:4).

Encouragement vs. Discouragement

A few years ago I was teaching this principle to a group of pastors in Melbourne, Australia. On one particular evening, we dedicated more than an hour to the issue of comfort in conjunction with prophetic utterance. After thoroughly explaining basic prophecy as edification, exhortation, and comfort, I then released the group to prophesy to each other. I instructed everyone to prophesy nothing but positive words of encouragement. My final instructions to them were, "Say nothing negative to anyone."

In spite of these instructions, someone prophesied to a young Christian that he had cancer. The frightened man who received this supposed encouragement stood in the middle of the sanctuary shaking like a leaf. I tried to console him, but my effort seemed to be hopeless. He left the meeting believing that he had terminal cancer. Just imagine what he might have felt! Even if he received a positive report from a doctor contradicting this negative word, he still suffered the pain of undue stress and worry.

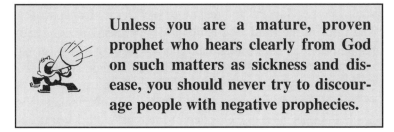

Unless you are a mature, proven prophet who hears clearly from God on such matters as sickness and disease, you should never try to discourage people with negative prophecies.

In light of this incident, I was further convinced that prophetic people should focus solely on edification, exhortation, and comfort. Unless you are a mature, proven prophet who hears clearly from God on such matters as sickness and disease, you should never discourage people with negative prophecies. It is not only unhealthy for others but also dangerous for you. There is a distinct possibility that the prophetic curses you speak could come back on you. Jesus said, "Judge not, that you be not judged. For with the judgment you pronounce you will be judged, and the measure you give will be the measure you get" (Mt. 7:1-2 RSV).

(Note: If you discern something negative about someone, remember, it is probably discernment of spirits or a word of knowledge, not the gift of prophecy.)

A friend of mine had an experience that illustrates this principle. Once, while ministering under a powerful anointing in a church service, my friend said some critical things about another ministry. The Lord sharply rebuked him for using his prophetic gifting, *especially under the anointing* and in a public setting, to criticize a fellow servant of Christ.

The Lord then told him that he had incurred judgment for that act and that the judgment would be one month of severe sickness and public silence for each minute of judgment (criticism of this other believer's ministry) spoken while under the anointing. The subsequent months were extremely difficult for him, as my friend faced a life-threatening illness. Then, after the prescribed period of time, he was healed and resumed his ministry. This example of my friend can serve as a warning to us young prophetic pups to use great caution while ministering under God's anointing.

aDVANceD propHeTic

As stated in the last chapter, basic prophetic purpose consists of edification, exhortation, and comfort. We also learned that this realm of prophecy is accessible to almost anyone who wishes to encourage the Church, even those who are beginners in prophecy. However, there are other areas of prophetic purpose that should be exercised only by those who are advanced in their gifting. These include conviction, impartation, direction, and foretelling (prediction).

Conviction

> *But if all prophesy, and an unbeliever or outsider enters, he is convicted by all, he is called to account by all, the secrets of his heart are disclosed; and so, falling on his face, he will worship God and declare that God is really among you* (1 Corinthians 14:24-25 RSV).

According to *Unger's Bible Dictionary*, page 219, conviction, as a legal term, means "to be found guilty." In everyday language it means "being persuaded or convinced." In a theological sense, it means "being convicted at the bar of one's own conscience as a sinner in view of God's law." The means by which this conviction comes are varied. It can be imparted through preaching, reading, and hearing the Word; meditation upon Scripture; heart reflection; or calamity. Occasionally, it comes through the prophetic.

When used to bring conviction, prophecy can be a powerful instrument in the hands of Christians. This is especially true for evangelism. For instance, a prophetic word of edification, exhortation, and comfort is usually sufficient for most believers. What sincere Christians need is encouragement, not false conviction. On the other hand, stronger measures (such as conviction through prophecy) are required to get the attention of unbelievers. As stated in First Corinthians 14: 24-25, when a prophetic word is used to expose the secrets of a person's heart, that person is then graced with an opportunity to humble himself and repent before God.

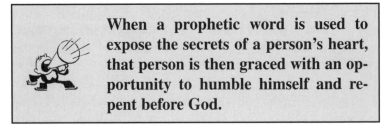

When a prophetic word is used to expose the secrets of a person's heart, that person is then graced with an opportunity to humble himself and repent before God.

Although Paul established the validity of these prophetic utterances that are given to bring conviction upon an unbeliever, it is interesting to note, however, that these verses in First Corinthians 14: 24-25 place the unbeliever inside the meeting place as opposed to outside in the marketplace. This might have been the case in Paul's day, but the percentage of unbelievers attending today's churches is much smaller. Therefore, it would not be unreasonable in today's world to apply a reversal of this Scripture. We can take the initiative and go to the unbelievers, as opposed to waiting for them to come to us. By invading their turf with the gift of prophecy, we give God the opportunity to bring conviction on their hearts through revealing intimate details of their lives.

What an incredible thought! Wouldn't it be great to walk up to a total stranger on the street and say something like: "Hi! God loves you so much that He has revealed some specific details of your life to me. He showed me that your name is Jim, you were born in May of 1950, you have three children, your wife recently left you, and you are prepared to commit suicide."

If these things were true, don't you think that this person would be shaken by your ability to have *read his mail*? Is it possible that he would acknowledge the loving power of an omniscient God who would give you such detailed information? According to First Corinthians 14: 24-25, this person would probably fall under the power of conviction and begin to worship God—affirming that God is with you.

This principle of evangelism through the prophetic is also seen in the Gospel of John. Upon receiving a prophetic word, a Samaritan woman declared Jesus to be the Messiah. This woman was not convicted by preaching, teaching, or miracles, but by the prophetic. John 4 describes the incident as follows:

> *The woman saith unto Him, Sir, give me this water, that I thirst not, neither come hither to draw. Jesus said unto her, Go, call thy husband, and come hither. The woman answered and said, I have no husband. Jesus said unto her, Thou hast well said, I have no husband: for thou hast had five husbands....The woman saith unto Him, Sir, I percieve that Thou art a prophet. ... The woman then left her waterpot, and went her way into the city, and saith to the men, Come, see a man, which told me all things that I ever did: is not this the Christ?* (John 4:15-19,28-29)

Why is this method of prophetic conviction so often under-utilized by the Church today? Several reasons come to mind. First, most evangelical and fundamentalist churches do not believe in the prophetic and, therefore, cannot emphasize its use as an evangelistic tool.

Second, those churches who do believe in the prophetic ministry seldom take it outside the walls of their sanctuaries. Due to a lack of confidence, which has hindered us from hearing and expressing the voice of God, we are afraid to exercise our gift in a public setting. We're so busy attempting to get our own needs and desires met that there is hardly any time left to pursue prophetic evangelism.

Finally, we have such an unhealthy desire to receive recognition from our peers that most believers value prophecy only when it is modeled on stage in front of other Christians. Seldom do we exhibit the desire to "take it to the streets."

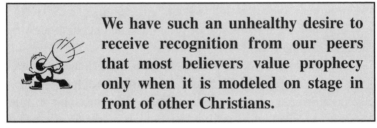

We have such an unhealthy desire to receive recognition from our peers that most believers value prophecy only when it is modeled on stage in front of other Christians.

In the near future these things are going to change. My hope is that thousands of prophetic people will flood the marketplace and job sites, bringing conviction through the gift of prophecy. I can almost envision a sign on the church door that states: "Sorry, this church is closed today. We've gone fishing for men."

Impartation

> *Do not neglect the gift you have, which was given you by prophetic utterance when the council of elders laid their hands upon you* (1 Timothy 4:14 RSV).

The underlying principle of *impartation* means "to share, bestow, or dispense something that has great value and substance." The means by which we impart something can be likened to dispensing electrical current. For example, electricity that is stored in a transformer can be retained, discharged, or sent to various places at will. The same is true of prophetic impartation. We, as believers, have the privilege of dispensing God's power to mankind.

You can only impart that which you possess. Therefore, people catch what you have, not what you say you have.

However, you can only impart that which you possess. For instance, if you have the measles and people hang around you long enough, they will eventually catch the measles. You can tell them a hundred times a day that you have the flu instead of the measles, but in spite of your confession, people will catch what you have, not what you say you have.

This principle most certainly applies to spiritual impartation. In First Timothy 4:14, a *gift* was imparted to Timothy through prophecy and the laying on of hands. We are not certain what this gift was, but obviously, he received a spiritual endowment that was resident within those who ministered to him. Simply stated: He caught what they possessed through the principle of impartation.

Other than Paul's reference to impartation in the Book of Timothy, are there other instances in Scripture where this dynamic of impartation is found? Indeed, the principle of impartation is demonstrated throughout much of the Bible. Jacob imparted various blessings to his 12 sons by the laying on of hands and by prophecy (Gen. 48–49). Moses, at the end of his ministry, prophesied over his servant, Joshua, and anointed him to lead Israel into the Promised Land (see Num. 27:18-23). And, most importantly, Jesus imparted His power to the 12 disciples who, as a result, healed the sick and raised the dead.

Does this mean that anyone can impart through the prophetic? Perhaps, but if you look closely at Timothy's experience, it was the elders who imparted the gift to him, not novices. Why? Because immature Christians usually lack the spiritual experience or stamina required to endow gifts upon the Church. It's true that they are capable of impartation, but what is imparted will often come from their souls and not from God's Holy Spirit. As a result, those who receive their ministry may walk away with a piece of the man, rather than a piece of God's Spirit.

Remember, only that which has been deposited in you by the Holy Spirit is worthy of being transferred. All else is hot air—vain words that produce nothing more than false hope and confusion. That is why prophetic impartation is not to be exercised by beginners. This ministry is a function that belongs to those advanced believers who are familiar with the dynamic of impartation.

On Fire

I have often seen the principle of impartation at work in my own ministry. One of the most vivid examples took place at a meeting in Los Angeles in the late 1980s. I was speaking at a prophetic conference when I noticed a group of four young people come through the door. Immediately, the Presence of God rose up within my spirit and prompted me to call them forward for personal ministry.

As they approached the platform, I felt impressed to prophesy concerning the secrets of their hearts. One by one, God began to reveal specific details about their lives through the word of knowledge. At this time, the prophetic word was so precise that the leader of this group fell on the floor and began to weep uncontrollably. Finally, when he had regained his composure, I laid my hands on the group and prophesied to them again. I declared that God would greatly use them, particularly in prophetic ministry.

Prior to that night, I had never seen these young people before. Furthermore, I had no idea that they were a rap, dance, and drama team who had been saved out of the Hollywood scene a few years earlier. Nor was I aware that they had little understanding of the prophetic. Nevertheless, I believed what God said and again affirmed them in their future ministries.

About a year later, I received a phone call from the pastor of a church concerning the young people I had prophesied over. He had asked this group (who called themselves *On Fire Ministries*) to speak in one of his meetings. The report he gave was absolutely astounding! Apparently, they ministered with an extremely high level of prophetic anointing, by calling out several members of his congregation by name and ministering to them in a specific manner. He further related that these young people had prophesied over some of his elders with an accuracy that greatly exceeded their spiritual maturity.

The next time I saw *On Fire Ministries*, I asked the obvious question: "What happened at my friend's church the other day?"

Rucky, the leader of the group, looked at me with a twinkle in his eye, and said with a smile, "You prophesied this stuff over me and I received it as from the Lord. So, when I was ministering at the church, I could sense your prophetic anointing and just said what I thought you would say to the people."

At first, the young man's explanation sounded a little weird to me. However, the more I thought about it, the more I realized what had taken place. The Spirit of God had used me to impart the prophetic to these young people a year earlier. As a result, what I possessed in the form of prophetic anointing was now operating in their lives. The dynamic of impartation enabled them to reap the fruit of another man's anointing and ministry.

Direction

> *...These disciples warned Paul—the Holy Spirit prophesying through them—not to go on to Jerusalem. ...a man named Agabus, who also had the gift of prophecy...took Paul's belt, bound his own feet and hands with it and said, "The Holy Spirit declares, 'So shall the owner of this belt be bound by the Jews in Jerusalem and turned over to the Romans'"* (Acts. 21:4,10-11 TLB).

Directional prophecy is also a vital aspect of the prophetic. Those who receive it have benefited tremendously. Those who reject it are often lost in a sea of uncertainty or, worse yet, find their lives in jeopardy. In the case of Paul's trip to Jerusalem, the latter was true. He was told by prophetic utterance not to make this particular voyage, yet he decided to go forward with his travel plans. Eventually, things developed just as they were prophesied. Upon his arrival in Jerusalem, he was resisted by the elders, bound, chained, and subjected to many abuses.

In contrast to Paul's experience, the Bible is filled with testimonies of people who benefited greatly from directional prophecy. As a result of prophetic guidance, people's lives were spared from certain death, aimless men came face to face with their destinies, nations were delivered from bondage, kingdoms were conquered, and great wars were won.

In other instances, God's people also found guidance in ordinary matters of life. In some instances it was whom to marry, what to say, and where to go. On one occasion, Hosea was directed by God to marry Gomer, the daughter of Diblaim (see Hos. 1:2-3). Samuel was instructed to speak specific prophetic words of judgment to King Saul (see 1 Sam. 15). Philip was told to go down to a desert place called Gaza where he ministered to an Ethopian eunuch (see Acts 8:26-40).

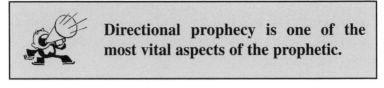

Directional prophecy is one of the most vital aspects of the prophetic.

In light of the many examples of prophetic direction in the Bible, there are those who still believe that directional prophecy is confined to the lives of Bible characters. However, I am convinced that the dynamic of prophetic guidance is still in operation today. Furthermore, I am also convinced that there are thousands of contemporary Christians who hear from God on various issues—great and small.

I personally have witnessed hundreds of situations in which believers' lives have been enhanced as a result of directional prophecy. They have benefited greatly on issues such as how to find one's ministry, where to build a church, when to buy a house, how long to stay in one place, and whom to trust.

In fairness to the critics, I have also heard horror stories about prophetic guidance. It seems that a number of Christians have been needlessly destroyed by so-called *directive utterances.* People were told to marry the wrong mate, divorce the right one, relocate to distant nations, invest in failing businesses, and do an assortment of other things that were not the will of God for them. Nevertheless, in my own experience, the directive words I have both received and given have been mostly profitable.

Personal Direction

One of my fondest memories concerning directive prophecy came as a result of a prophetic word given to me by a man named Brother Mitchell. Before I met this old prophet, I was in total confusion about the direction of my life. I had a young family, no money, a call to the ministry, and a great desire to attend a Bible institute.

A friend who had heard about this dear man of God insisted that we drive to his house in hope of receiving a prophetic word. I was reluctant at first, but eventually agreed to make the trip. When we arrived, the old prophet greeted us at the door with a smile worthy of an angel. He graciously asked us into his little house and quickly arranged two chairs for us. What followed changed the course of my life.

Before I could sit down, this wonderful old prophet began to prophesy over me. He said, "I see a young man with a family. He has no finances. He is called to ministry and has been praying about going to Bible school."

He then leaned forward, looked deep into my eyes, and said, "Son, it is not God's will at this time for you to go to Bible school. It's true you are called, but God wants to personally train you. That which He has for you to do cannot be learned at Bible school. Soon God will open a door of ministry and you will see His financial provision. So stand still and see the salvation of your God."

He then smiled, opened his Bible, and began to give me further instruction on other issues related to my life. When he had finished, I knew that I had glimpsed the will of God for my life and ministry.

Hardly two months passed before things began to fall in line with the prophecy I had received. It became impossible for me to go to Bible school, and, as a result, I was offered a position as a staff minister at a local church. From that point on, God began to develop my ministry according to the word spoken over me. To this day, I am still strengthened and guided by the words of this godly old man who understood the value of giving and receiving directional prophecy.

He also instructed me that it is best to refrain from directive prophecy, unless you are fully developed in this gift. If you are in error, you will bear the responsibility and judgment that comes from sending God's sheep down the wrong path.

To Foretell

> *"...The prophets have inquired and searched diligently, who prophesied of the grace that should come unto you"* (1 Peter 1:10).

Foretelling is the predictive element of prophecy. Its roots are in the Messianic predictions found in the Old Testament. Many of these prophecies given by old covenant prophets spoke of things yet to come, especially the earthly ministry of our Lord Jesus (see Deut. 18:15; Mt. 3:11). In less significant matters, other prophets foretold events such as floods, droughts, famines, economic failures, and wars. Jesus, the greatest prophet of all time, gave us prophetic insight into things that transcend the life span of our globe. He prophesied about future times, eons of years to come.

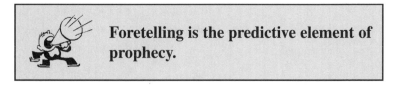

Foretelling is the predictive element of prophecy.

In much the same way, *predictive prophecy* operates in prophetic ministry today. Many present-day prophets have accurately foretold such things as the birth of babies, the election of future presidents, the fall of immoral ministries, imminent airplane crashes, floods, earthquakes, and other major events.

I have seen these kinds of prophecies fulfilled in my own ministry. With the help of God, I was able to warn the church about the San Francisco earthquake of 1990. Seven days before it occurred, I released a prophetic statement detailing the time and

Richter scale reading of the quake. This prophecy was spoken at Newport Beach Vineyard Christian Fellowship in Newport Beach, California.

Also, the great floods of 1993 began only a few months after God prompted me to prophesy about a great deluge of water that would bring destruction to parts of this nation. I prophesied this in a radio interview that was broadcast by station KTYM in Los Angeles on January 1, 1993. To the surprise of my critics, both of these prophecies came to pass as detailed. It was clear that "surely the Lord God does nothing, without revealing His secret to His servants the prophets" (Amos 3:7 RSV).

In spite of the evidence, however, many people still question God's willingness to reveal such things to His people. They just can't believe that God can speak today and that revelation knowledge of future events are tokens of God's grace, designed to strengthen our faith in an all-knowing Creator.

In certain religious circles it is also debatable whether or not these tokens of revelation are critical for survival today. However, in the days to come, I believe that prophetic impressions will serve as warnings to prepare us for the great calamities that are approaching Planet Earth. Remember, the Scripture is replete with example after example of how God used His prophetic spokesmen to save and deliver God's people and the world. Therefore, the issue is not whether God is willing to reveal His purpose to mankind, but whether or not we are willing to train up this new generation of prophets to hear the voice of God and dispense His saving knowledge to the nations.

Chapter Eight

HOW TO receive propHeTic revelation

No two people are exactly the same. We all have the same basic design, but under no circumstances do we feel, reason, act, or think in the exact same way. Unequivocally speaking, we are unique expressions of God.

This uniqueness is often seen in the way we respond to outward stimuli. For example, three different people might attend a musical concert and have three different reactions. The first person might find the experience uplifting because of the refreshing rhythm of the music. The second one might be irritated by the beat and volume of the music and hear nothing but loud noise. The third could be so touched by the words of the song that he or she is oblivious to the music. They all heard from the same source but received and responded differently.

Unequivocally speaking, we are unique expressions of God. Therefore, the way we receive from God varies according to the uniqueness of our personality, emotions, and spiritual makeup.

The same is true of the spiritual realm. The way we receive from God varies according to the uniqueness of our personality, emotions, and spiritual makeup. The truth is, God didn't create Christian clones who respond as preprogrammed robots. Instead, He created us divinely distinct, as independent life forms who hear from the Creator on different spiritual frequencies. And, because we are unique in this reception, we have the freedom to interpret incoming revelation in a way that is compatible with our understanding.

This principle of reception and interpretation is much like radio broadcasting and receiving. According to the 1983 edition of the *Lexicon Universal Encyclopedia* (volume 16, page 44), a radio tower transmits energy in the form of radio waves. These radio waves carrying specific information travel at the speed of light (186,000 miles per second). When the waves arrive at a receiving antenna, a small electrical voltage is produced. After this voltage has been amplified, the original information contained in the radio waves is retrieved and presented in an understandable form—the sound that comes from a loudspeaker, a picture on a television, or a printed page from a teletype machine.

God operates like a transmitting tower that broadcasts day and night. His Spirit is like radio waves that carry vital information. And, as believers, we are His receiving antennae awaiting a signal from Heaven.

This same principle also applies to prophetic reception. For example, God operates like a transmitting tower that broadcasts day and night. His Spirit is like radio waves that carry vital information. And, as believers, we are His receiving antenna awaiting a signal from Heaven. Therefore, whether we know it or not, we all receive prophetic transmissions from God, which are then translated into different forms such as visions, dreams, and impressions. The form this information takes depends on the specific equipment within our spiritual house, i.e., the frequency we are tuned into and the position of our antennae.

Therefore, since we receive in different ways, it would be foolish to stereotype the way Christians hear and receive from God. Remember, the way we interpret prophetic communication is not the standard for everyone. We should never expect others to operate exclusively on our particular frequency or understand completely the way God communicates with us. In the light of this diversity, we will investigate a few of the more common ways we receive revelation.

Visions

One of the ways we receive prophetic *communication* is through visions. The English words *vision* and *visions* are referred to more than 100 times in the Old and New Testaments. The root meaning is "to perceive or see." *Unger's Bible Dictionary* (page 1159) defines a vision as "a supernatural presentation of certain scenery or circumstances to the mind of a person while awake." Other references suggest that visions are "inspired insight of revelation from God."

My definition of visions is similar. I am convinced there is a point in time when supernatural perception merges with natural perception. While in our conscious state, we see images superimposed over our eyesight. It is much like peering through a powerful telescope and seeing things that are undetectable by the naked eye. Some say this phenomenon is enhanced by prayer and fasting. Others say that it is initiated by the sovereign will of God. Whatever position we take, one thing is certain. Like Paul, we too can "come to visions and revelations of the Lord" (2 Cor. 12:1).

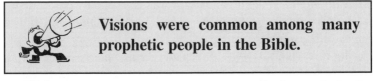

Visions were common among many prophetic people in the Bible.

Visions were common among many prophetic people in the Bible. In the Old Testament it is recorded that "the Lord came unto Abram in a vision" (Gen. 15:1). Balaam spoke of himself as having seen "the vision of the Almighty" (Num. 24:4). Samuel "feared to show Eli the vision" (1 Sam. 3:15). Isaiah referred to his writings as "the vision of Isaiah the son of Amoz" (Is. 1:1). Ezekiel declared, "The spirit took me up, and brought me in a vision by the Spirit of God" (Ezek. 11:24). Daniel had "visions of his head upon his bed" (see Dan. 4:13). Habakkuk was told, "Write the vision, and make it plain" (Hab. 2:2).

The New Testament informs us that Zacharias, the father of John the Baptist, also saw "a vision in the temple" (Lk. 1:22). Peter, James, and John saw a vision of Jesus standing with Moses and Elijah and were told, "Tell the vision to no man" (Mt. 17:9). Peter declared that while "in a trance I saw a vision" (Acts 11:5). At Troas, "a vision appeared to Paul in the night" (Acts 16:9). And lastly, John the Revelator declared, "I saw the horses in the vision" (Rev. 9:17).

Like their biblical counterparts, many present-day Christians have supernatural visions. It's not uncommon for them to receive visions that contain warnings, prophetic messages, predictions, and insight into the realm of heavenly things. Some have had visions of apocalyptic judgment and have seen grandiose imagery of Jesus and His Kingdom. Others have visions relating to the everyday affairs of life.

Visions have also played a significant role in shaping my life and ministry. One of these visions came at a very critical time in my life. Around 1985, I was desperately seeking God concerning His geographical will for my family and me. There were several options open to me, but I wasn't sure which location was right. One night, while praying about this matter, I fell asleep shortly after midnight. Three hours later, I was awakened with the sense of God's Presence within the room. I immediately fell into a multi-dimensional vision.

In this vision, I was physically lying in my bedroom in Arkansas while at the same time viewing the West Coast from a very great height. Suddenly, what I discerned to be an angel came and stood at my right side and pointed to the coastline. The angel said, "*This is where God wants you. Obey God and live; disobey God and die.*" These words were repeated two more times—then the vision disappeared.

Needless to say, I obeyed the vision. Not long after that night, I packed my family into our little car and headed west. I had more than 1,300 miles to travel and less than $500 in my pocket. To complicate matters, there was no church or ministry awaiting our arrival. All I possessed was my family, faith in God, and the memory of a searing vision that had been etched into my brain. When we arrived in California, God began to bless us because of our obedience to this heavenly vision.

Dreams

The *Lexicon Universal Encyclopedia* (1983 edition, volume 6, page 266) describes dreams as follows:

> "A dream is a series of images and ideas that occur during sleep. It appears that most dreams are connected with physical states, and that their psychological origin lies mainly in the region beneath 'the threshold of consciousness.' A majority of these dreams seem to reflect events, thoughts and feelings of the previous day or days. Dream content, in the natural, is a dynamic mixture derived from current events and past experiences, interests and urges."

Many dreams do not convey a real message to the dreamer. As Solomon says in Ecclesiastes 5:3, these dreams come "through the multitude of business." They are natural in origin and have no spiritual significance. On the other hand, sometimes dreams do carry specific messages from God. These dreams are supernaturally inspired and should be interpreted and applied to our lives.

To discern between natural dreams and supernatural dreams, a simple test can be used. Does the dream provoke you to pray and seek God? Is there a sense of God's Presence in the dream or immediately following the dream? While in the middle of dreaming are you aware that the dream is from God? Is the dream repeated over and over again? Is the dream symbolic or cryptic? Is Scripture seen or spoken in the dream? Does the dream wake you abruptly? Does the dream keep coming to mind for days or weeks? If you can say, "yes," to one or more of these questions, there is a strong possibility your dream is inspired by the Spirit of God.

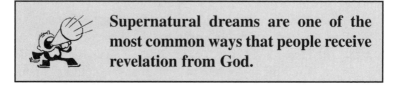

Supernatural dreams are one of the most common ways that people receive revelation from God.

Supernatural dreams are one of the most common ways that people receive revelation from God. In both Old and New Testament Scriptures, we find great significance attached to certain dreams. Jacob received blessing from the Lord through a dream. Joseph was given insight into his future as a result of a dream. By the telling of a dream, Gideon's army found strength to conquer the Midianites. Daniel, who was known as an interpreter of dreams, saw future events in a number of dreams. The angel of the Lord appeared to Joseph in a dream, telling him about the supernatural birth of Jesus. Apparently it was in a dream that the angel of God instructed Paul concerning the fate of those who were traveling with him to Rome. (See Genesis 28:11-15; 37:5-7; Judges 7:13; Daniel 7:1; Matthew 1:20-21; Acts 27:23-24.)

As a prophetic person, I, too, have been given many supernatural dreams. Even so, most of these dreams were given for the edification of the Church, not for my own use. On numerous occasions, I have walked into the pulpit armed with prophetic information that I received in a dream the night before. At times, I have had foreknowledge about the ebb and flow of the meeting, the spiritual state of the leaders, and a sensitivity to the secrets of strangers who were in attendance. As a result of this dream-knowledge, I've been able to impart comfort and direction to those who were in need.

One of the clearest examples of receiving prophetic information through a dream happened to me a few years ago. The night before I was scheduled to speak at a church in Los Angeles, I dreamed that I was already in the meeting. In the dream I was prophesying to people whom I had never seen before. Suddenly, I stopped and directed my attention to a young man on the end of the fifth row. I could clearly see his features, nationality, and the kind of clothes he was wearing. I paused for a moment, then said to him, *"Your name is Howard and I have a message from God for you."* For the next few minutes in the dream, I prophesied concerning the secrets of his heart.

The next morning I awoke from the dream and prepared to go to the meeting. When I arrived, I was whisked to the pulpit and properly introduced. I preached for about 45 minutes and then began to minister prophetically. Suddenly, I remembered the dream I had the night before. I turned and looked at the end of the fifth row. As I anticipated, the man I saw in the dream was sitting there smiling at me. He wore the same expression and the same clothes I had seen the night before. With a pounding heart, I said to him, "You don't know me, but I have already met you. Your name is Howard; stand up and receive the word of the Lord." Stunned, he stood sobbing to hear a word from a God who knew him by name.

Intuition/Impressions

Intuition has been described as knowledge that is arrived at spontaneously, without conscious steps of reasoning or inquiry. The expression, "I have an impression from the Lord," is Christian rhetoric that is similar in meaning to intuition but different in theory and application. For many Christians, the two are synonymous. For others, they are quite different. So, in fairness to each side we will discuss both intuition and impressions. We will begin with impressions.

 By embracing the redemptive work of Jesus, who is the second Adam, intuition can also be reclaimed, sanctified, and used for the Kingdom of God.

Throughout our lifetime, we receive thousands of intuitive thoughts. No one is exempt. Although our intuitiveness is expressed in different forms—having a gut feeling, having a sixth sense, being suddenly aware, or just having a feeling about something—this phenomenon can be experienced by sinner and saint alike.

In most cases, people react to these intuitive impressions with statements like, "Oh, I guess that was just me," or "I wonder where that thought came from." Usually, they dismiss this gut feeling, not knowing that it is often an accurate impression of things that are unknowable to them at the time.

Others believe, however, that our intuition is relegated to the realm of the flesh and the devil. They often warn believers of the dangers incurred when they dabble in this so-called *forbidden power*. They are convinced that intuition, as a latent power of the soul, should forever remain dormant and undeveloped.

They believe that Adam in his original state possessed a godly form of intuition; but as a result of his sin, this power fell out of its spiritual sphere and into the realm of man's soul, a domain where satan is believed to have access and influence. Due to this fallen state, they also teach that Adam's descendants now possess a perverted form of intuition. Therefore, the use of this fallen power is off-limits to everyone but satan, sorcerers, and fortunetellers.

In contrast to this teaching, I believe all things are redeemable in God. I am deeply convinced that things lost or perverted through the fall of Adam can be restored to their original intent. I am persuaded that by embracing the redemptive work of Jesus, who is the second Adam, intuition can also be reclaimed, sanctified, and used for the Kingdom of God. This principle is relatively simple: God gave it. Adam lost it. Satan perverted it. Jesus reclaimed it at Calvary. Christians now possess a sanctified soul.

This is not to say, however, that all intuition is good. For instance, intuitive people such as psychics, New Agers, clairvoyants, and fortunetellers operate in a realm of divination, not in a legitimate realm of the Holy Spirit. Therefore, it is absolutely impossible for them to have a sanctified intuition.

Impressions/Perception

As already mentioned, the statement, "I have an impression," is nothing more than contemporary Christian slang. The word *impression*, as it is currently used by Christians, is neither found in Scripture nor in the English dictionary. Therefore, under such circumstances it would be more appropriate to say, "The Lord has made me aware" or "I perceive by the Spirit of God."

Unlike the word *impression*, the word *perceived* is used several places in the New Testament. In one instance Jesus "*perceived* in His spirit" the thoughts of the scribes (Mk. 2:8). Elsewhere, when dealing with the disciples of the Pharisees, He "*perceived* their wickedness" (Mt. 22:18). When Peter was addressing Simon the sorcerer he said, "I *perceive* that thou art in the gall of bitterness" (Acts 8:23). Paul, while sailing on a ship from Alexandria said to those on board with him, "Sirs, I *perceive* that this voyage will be with hurt and much damage" (Acts 27:10).

This concept of prophetic perception is a common occurrence in the lives of most prophetic people today. In my own experience, some of the most accurate information I have received has come as a result of this principle. You can call it "redeemed intuition," "sanctified gut feelings," or "spirit awareness," but the bottom line is this: God has heightened my awareness to things around me. By virtue of this dynamic, I have developed a sensitivity to the inner nudging of the Holy Spirit. This has enabled me to perceive such things as imminent danger, hidden illness, secret sins, and the thoughts and intents of people's hearts. From time to time, these impressions have been helpful to both the Church and my community.

An example of this sort occurred some years ago at a supermarket where I had gone to shop for groceries. While walking past a couple of well-dressed men, I suddenly became aware of their evil intentions. In spite of their businesslike appearance, I perceived they were criminals who intended to rob the store once it closed. Trusting that my prophetic perception was accurate, I took a good hard look at their features and then left the premises. The next morning the local newspaper reported that a robbery had occurred at that store. Instantly, I called the police and gave them a full description of the two men I had seen the night before. As a result, they were quickly apprehended and charged with the crime.

Inner Voice/Audible Voice

Mental institutions are full of people who hear inner and audible voices. In some cases these voices are heard by those with brain disorders or those who have abused certain drugs. Although the medical community rarely agrees with me, I believe many of these voices come from the realm of spiritual darkness. In certain instances, these manifestations are nothing more than evil spirits who mimic human voice and speech.

In obedience to these diabolical voices, thousands of people have committed disgusting acts of violence. They have been instructed by these entities to rape, torture, murder, and commit suicide. To further complicate matters, these wicked spirits often insist that their commands are the "voice of God." Those who yield to these delusions are not only convinced that they hear from God, but also occasionally believe that they, themselves, are God.

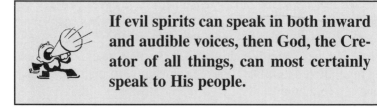

If evil spirits can speak in both inward and audible voices, then God, the Creator of all things, can most certainly speak to His people.

As a result of this deception, a person who dares to say he has heard from God runs the risk of being labeled an insane person. Yet, contrary to the belief of the skeptics, all supernatural voices do not come from satan. There are thousands of Christians who truly hear from God and are led by His voice. And why not? If evil spirits can speak in both inward and audible voices, then God, the Creator of all things, can most certainly speak to His people. Jesus substantiated this truth when He stated in John 10:27, "My sheep hear My voice." In Revelation 3:20 the resurrected Christ again declares, "If any man hear My voice, and open the door, I will come in to him."

In other instances in Scripture, the voice of the Lord is referred to over 125 times. Our ancestors, Adam and Eve, "heard the voice of the Lord" (Gen. 3:8). At Jerusalem, Peter relates his encounter with God and declared, "I heard a voice saying unto me, Arise, Peter" (Acts 11:7). As Paul recounted his conversion on the Damascus Road, he stated, "I heard a voice speaking unto me, and saying in the Hebrew tongue, Saul, Saul" (Acts 26:14). In the Book of Revelation, John writes that he also heard, "a great voice" (Rev. 1:10).

It's apparent that the voice of the Lord comes to Christians in two forms, inward and audible. In the Scriptures previously mentioned, the latter form usually was used. Those to whom God spoke in this manner seemed to hear an audible voice with their natural ears. It was not an inner sense or impression that they received, but the voice of God, which was manifest in the natural realm of hearing.

Although I rarely hear God in this fashion, I know several prophetic men who do. I have a friend named Bob who has had countless experiences of this kind. He is not crazy or weird as some may think. Rather, he is a highly sensitive prophetic person who is tuned to a spiritual frequency uncommon to most Christians. As a result of this special sensitivity, there are seasons in his life when he hears the audible voice of God on a daily basis. Many of his friends liken Bob to a modern-day Ezekiel.

Should we who are prophetic expect to hear God in this fashion? Perhaps, but Bob and others like him are more of an exception than a rule. Most prophetic people today rarely hear the audible voice of God. Usually it is an inner voice that speaks to us as the oracle of God. To some, this inner voice is defined as God speaking through their spirits. To others, it is God speaking to their minds. However, the prophet Elijah simply described it as a "still small voice" (1 Kings 19:12).

In any case, no matter what your definition of inner voice is, one thing is certain. Many contemporary Christians are divinely led by an *inner nudging* or *whispering* of the Holy Spirit. These inner impressions of God's voice have encouraged the down-hearted, given direction to those in need of guidance, and protected those who are in danger. More than once, my own life has been spared because I heeded the inner voice of God.

Mental Pictures

Another common way that people receive the prophetic is through mental pictures. These pictures are much like the images seen in the subconscious mind while dreaming, yet they come while awake. They are clearer than dreams but not as vivid as visions, lying somewhere between the realm of natural eyesight and conscious thought. They are often referred to as *seeing with the mind's eye*.

Many times mental pictures come without warning or fore-thought. In the same way that a camera's eye momentarily opens to capture a particular scene, the mind's eye gives us snapshots of past, present, and future images. In a split second, things can be perceived that are unrelated to one's present state of mind. These pictures can come in Technicolor or in black and white, in clear form or in abstract images.

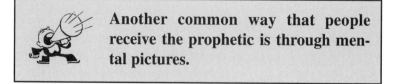

Another common way that people receive the prophetic is through mental pictures.

I have talked to scores of people who have experienced the phenomena of mental pictures at one time or another. In some cases, these pictures pertain to the everyday, ordinary matters of life. In other instances, they are a bit less common. For instance, some people have mental pictures of unexpected guests ringing their doorbells prior to their actual arrival. They have also seen, in their mind's eye, a telephone ringing only seconds before it actually occurs. Others experience mental flashes relating to matters of greater importance, such as imminent danger, political and social changes, devastating weather patterns, and economic collapse.

However, whether these visions seem important or insignificant, remember, there are many dangers associated with the process of receiving and interpreting the meaning and source of mental pictures. Upon perceiving an imminent catastrophic event such as an earthquake, flood, or accident, what must we do with it? More importantly, how can we discern its origin? Is this mental picture from God? Is it an aberration of the mind? Or is it negative imagery sent by the devil?

Many of these answers depend upon our spiritual position in Christ. If we truly believe that we have the mind of Christ, then we need to confidently explore the possibility that these images may have actually been given to us by God. If we are uncertain about the spiritual state of our minds, then we must disregard these images until a time when we are confident that we are operating with the mind of Christ.

Conclusion

Finally, it's not good enough to just receive and discern revelation. We must also become wise stewards of that which God has deposited within us. Christians who receive revelation by way of dreams, visions, mental imagery, and the voice of God must learn how to develop and dispense that knowledge in a way that is pleasing to God. We will examine this issue of stewardship in the following chapter.

Chapter Nine

STEWARDSHIP OF THE PROPHETIC

Many Christians today aspire to prophetic ministry. Some will achieve this goal and develop a fruitful ministry; others will not. Those who fail will attempt to place the blame on either of two things: God's restraint or satan's resistance. Occasionally, the fault may lie with Heaven or hell but, as a rule, most Christians are disqualified from ministry because of their own selfish motives, not because of God or satan.

> **Most Christians are disqualified from ministry because of their own selfish motives, not because of God or satan.**

This is especially true of selfish Christians who are consumed with an insatiable desire to be ministered unto. Like a giant sponge, many of these "bless me believers" absorb every drop of spiritual water that issues forth from the wellspring of the Church. When others are ministering, these sheep are the first in line to receive. They are receivers not givers, reservoirs not channels.

In contrast, Jesus, the greatest prophet of all times, said in Matthew 20:28, "…the Son of man came not to be ministered unto, but to minister…." In much the same way, those of us who wish to be blessed with success in ministry today must understand that *it is more blessed to give than to receive.* We must cease to look for a *word* for ourselves and become a *word* to others. We must realize that God doesn't want to speak to us as much as He wants to speak *through* us.

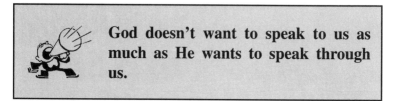

> **God doesn't want to speak to us as much as He wants to speak through us.**

It is, therefore, imperative that we consider others before ourselves. Regardless of our own needs and desires, we must attempt to unselfishly feed and nurture the Body of Christ. Once we have recognized this fundamental principle of giving first and receiving last, then we can begin to develop a solid base for ministry.

Giving out of Obedience

In addition to selfless giving, we must administer prophetic words with an attitude of obedience and faith. *We must simply obey what God says to do and believe that He is responsible for the results.*

This principle of obedience was clearly illustrated to me some years ago. At the end of a very low-key meeting, I began to minister prophetically to a group of people who had gathered at the front of the church. There didn't seem to be much anointing present that day, but out of obedience to my calling I continued to press forward with ministry. I systematically prophesied according to the measure of faith that I possessed.

At the end of the prayer line, I noticed a woman who seemed eager to receive from God. I didn't know what she needed, but the Spirit seemed to say, "Prophesy to her head." As I approached her reluctantly, I thought: *How can I prophesy to someone's head? What am I to say? Do I say, "You have a round head, two ears and a nose"?* I must admit that such a prophecy was tempting, but of course, that is not what I said. After much consideration, I turned, pointed my finger at her head, and prophesied a familiar Scripture. The prophecy went something like this: "The Lord is thy glory and the lifter of your head and He anoints your head with oil."

When I had finished the prophecy, I paused and waited for a response. Nothing seemed to happen, so I left the room as quickly as possible. I felt dejected and discouraged. I thought that I had missed God. I left vowing never to do that sort of thing again!

A few days later, I received a phone call from the conference coordinator. His first words were, "I want to tell you what happened the other day. The woman whose head you prophesied over was completely healed of a brain tumor." He went on to say that the lady had been scheduled for surgery, but after the prophecy she went to the hospital for another X-ray. Much to the surprise of her doctor, the tumor had completely disappeared.

I was bewildered by this report. I remember thinking: *How could this be? I didn't have the faith for such a miracle, nor did I understand what I had prophesied.* Then I remembered the story in John chapter 2 where Jesus turned water into wine. Suddenly it became clear. Like those at the feast who were obedient to draw water out of their vessel and give it away, I, too, had been faithful to do my part. As a result, the Lord was also faithful to do His part. In obedience, I had given the water of the word, and Jesus had turned it into spiritual wine.

Starting Simple

Undoubtedly, the principle of obedient giving is essential to the development of the prophetic. Yet, once we begin to flow in prophetic ministry, it is important that we do not run ahead of our gifting. Our spiritual output should never exceed our spiritual input. If this happens, we are well on our way to failure.

It's important that we do not run ahead of our gifting. Our spiritual output should never exceed our spiritual input.

In many instances, those who are newcomers to prophecy are convinced they have an anointing equivalent to that of the prophet Elijah. However, after allowing them to float upon this cloud of fantasy for a while, God eventually clips their wings. Like falling stars, they come crashing down to earth and find themselves face to face with the real measure of their gift. Although, they envision themselves prophesying like Elijah or Jeremiah at Sunday morning service, when they stand to speak the prophecy, it comes out like this: *"Thus saith the Lord...aah, aah...I think that, maybe...aah,aah...possibly...aah...that God is here. Oh, and ...aah...He loves you, too."*

Again, you can only give what you have, not what you might think you have. For this reason, only an unwise steward would withdraw more money out of an account than has been deposited. The same can be applied to prophetic people. If we minister beyond our means, we run the risk of spiritual bankruptcy. God will close our account. When we attempt to make a large prophetic withdrawal, the check will bounce, embarrassing both ourselves and the Church. Consequently, we have no choice but to humble ourselves and give out what we have, not what we were hoping for. This contribution may be small and simple, but, like the aforementioned prophecy, it's real spiritual tender and will be honored by the bank of Heaven.

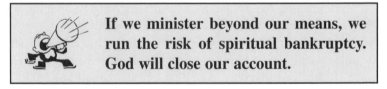

If we minister beyond our means, we run the risk of spiritual bankruptcy. God will close our account.

Sticking to the Basics

When prophesying, it's better to be simple and real rather than complex and phony. In most cases, a basic affirmation of God's love and protection does more for a Christian's outlook than all the hyper prophecies that could hurtle him into the outer limits of spiritual space. As a result of a simple prophecy, I have seen backsliders return to Christ, hopeless people saved from sui-cide, and countless numbers of oppressed Christians receive comfort and encouragement.

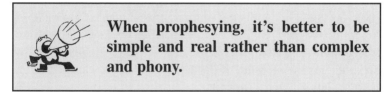

When prophesying, it's better to be simple and real rather than complex and phony.

Not long ago, I heard a story that illustrates the value of *simple* prophetic words. A visitor from another country was driving a car down a U.S. highway. To reach his destination, the man had to travel on an unfamiliar road. At the beginning of his trip he noticed a gigantic sign over the freeway that read "Interstate 10." At first the man was confident of his direction. But after travel-ing for a while, he became concerned that he might be driving down the wrong highway. The further he drove, the more anxious he became.

Finally, his fears were put to rest by a little sign on the side of the road that read, "You are still on Interstate 10." In relating this to a friend, he said, "I really like the great big signs over the freeway that tell me which way to go. But most of all I appreciate the lit-tle signs that let me know I am still going in the right direction."

Isn't that the way it is in Christian life? In the beginning, we all need the big signs from God. As new converts, our faith in the Lord seems to be dependent upon heavy prophetic words, Technicolor visions, and spiritually inspired dreams. Yet, when the light of revelation fades with the passing of time, we learn to respect the little signs that come our way. When someone reminds us that *"I the Lord am with you always. I will never leave you nor forsake you. This is the way; walk ye in it,"* we're so grateful that we often fall on our faces to thank God for these simple words of confirmation.

Starting at the Bottom

Prophetic people must refine their prophetic skills by starting at the bottom. For example, everyone would agree that you don't begin as a musician by first playing at Carnegie Hall. Neither do you start a prophetic ministry by prophesying on stage in front of the whole church. You must simply begin at the bottom, and through patience and practice, your gift will eventually make room for you. (Remember: *The Almighty God builds us line upon line and precept upon precept.* Then, after we have proven ourselves faithful in small things, He exposes us to greater visibility and enlarges the measure of our talents and gifts. This is true for both leaders and their sheep.)

The same was true of many men in the Bible. Great heroes of the faith such as Moses, David, and Joseph began their ministries after years of secret, behind-the-scenes training. In the case of Moses, the miracles that he performed came as a result of 40 long years of breaking, training, and development—starting at the bottom. Moses yielded to God's process long before he wielded God's power.

Moses yielded to God's process before he wielded God's power.

Likewise, the psalmist David ascended to the throne of Israel only after he had spent decades practicing his gift in obscure places. Although he was gifted and anointed as a child, the realization of his calling came through the process of time. David's faithfulness to God's process made him one of the most notable warriors and kings of all times.

Joseph's life and ministry is also a timeless example of what it means to start at the bottom. Due to his prophetic gift, the young lad was cast into a well by his brothers and then sold into slavery. Later, while in Egypt, he further developed his prophetic gift at the bottom of a prison. For more than a decade he served God in obscurity, faithfully practicing his gift on fellow slaves and prisoners (see Gen. 37,39–41).

Then, when the process of time had matured the young dreamer and his gift, the Lord placed him in Egypt's spotlight.

The king was so impressed with Joseph's gift that he made him ruler over all the land. Like that of Moses and David, Joseph's ministry flourished from his willingness to be faithful in the small things, *beginning at the bottom.*

The Process of Development

The references made to Moses, David, and Joseph are vital examples designed to counterbalance the impatient nature so characteristic of contemporary Christians. In an age of instant everything, we have developed a Christian culture that relies on immediacy rather than intimacy. Like impatient children with a drive-thru mentality, we want it all and we want it right now.

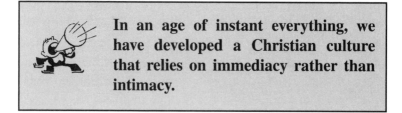

In an age of instant everything, we have developed a Christian culture that relies on immediacy rather than intimacy.

Perhaps in our rush and confusion we have failed to comprehend the words of a wise man, who said in Ecclesiastes 3:1, "To every thing there is a season, and a time to every purpose under the heaven." We have forgotten that we live in a realm where trees are grown, fruit is matured in its season, and babies develop according to the process of time.

Therefore, those who have received spiritual gifts, especially prophetic gifts, must remember several important things. First, there is a process of development that we must all endure. In order to mature our gifts, we must be subject to God's time and seasons. While in this formative process, we must not become impatient and despise that which God has planted in us.

Second, when God is developing our gift, we must not minister beyond the level of our maturity. We must be willing to operate with the measure of grace God has given us—in simple ways and in obscure places. If we are not ready to stand before kings, then, like Joseph, we must continue to practice our gift at the bottom of the prison.

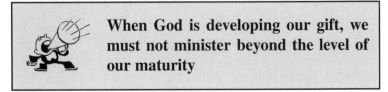

When God is developing our gift, we must not minister beyond the level of our maturity

Third, if we learn to be patient while in the growth process, things will be much easier for us and for the Church. We will feel less compelled to minister in front of a congregation or to prophesy over notable people.

And, finally, if we use our prophetic gift to encourage people outside of a church setting, our ministries will begin to flourish on a daily basis.

Chapter Ten

prophecy anD THe CHUrCH

It has been said that a picture is worth a thousand words. Recently, while thumbing through a Christian magazine, I came across a cartoon that clearly expressed a major problem within the Church. In this cartoon a lamb and a shepherd were squared off, face to face, ready to enter mortal combat with one another.

The lamb wore boxing gloves and was standing erect on his hind legs with both hands raised in defiance. Towering over the lamb was an angry shepherd who had his staff drawn back in a combat position, much like that of a samurai warrior. Although both seemed reluctant to start the fight, it was apparent that each one was capable of defending himself from the advances of the other. The caption over the picture should have read, "Go ahead. I dare you to hit me first."

This cartoon reflects the present conflict that exists between prophetic sheep and pastoral leadership. Only deliberate ignorance would prevent anyone from admitting that a serious breach

Most prophetic people avoid pastors as though they have the plague. Likewise, most pastors are relieved when prophetic people leave their churches.

has developed between these two groups. So great is this breach that most prophetic people avoid pastors as though they had the plague. Likewise, most pastors are relieved when prophetic people leave their churches.

Why has this breach festered into an almost incurable wound? On the one hand, the pastor feels offended because the prophetic person is reluctant to come under church authority. On the contrary, the prophetic person feels threatened by harsh treatment, which he interprets as a pastor's over-controlling abuse of authority. The result is a relational standoff, a no-win situation for either side.

As one who has pastored several churches and traveled in an itinerant prophetic ministry, I understand the inner fears of both sides. For the pastor who is committed to scriptural balance, moderation, body life, and biblical submission, it is extremely hard to embrace a prophetic person who seems to be mystical, free-spirited, independent, and extreme in the area of revelation.

For the prophetic person who feels an obligation to protect his ministry, it is equally hard to submit himself or his gift to the jurisdiction of pastoral oversight. This is especially true if the pastor appears to be intolerant, unapproachable, and skeptical of the prophetic. Consequently, both feel rejected by the other, making it difficult to maintain a working relationship.

Identifying Valid Prophetic Ministry

Before a healing of the breach between the prophetic and pastoral ministries can happen, there must first be an understanding of the roles played by each party. The prophetic person must understand the dynamics of pastoral function, and the pastor must understand the dynamics of the prophetic. Most importantly, both must recognize the role of the other as *vital* to the Church.

In keeping with the theme of this book, however, we will not explore the function of the pastoral office. Our concern is strictly related to the role and operation of prophetic ministry within the Body of Christ. In order to define this ministry and its relationship to the Church, I have divided the prophetic into four basic levels:

1. The spirit of prophecy
2. The gift of prophecy
3. The prophetic mantle
4. The office of prophet

The first level, pertains to the spirit of prophecy and is the most common form of prophetic utterance in the Church. According to Revelation 19:10, this manifestation of prophecy is the same as the testimony of Jesus Christ. In specific terms, level one consists of an anointing of the Holy Spirit that enables people who are not prophets or who do not possess a prophetic gift to prophesy. When this form of prophetic anointing falls upon a group of people, even backsliders have been known to prophesy with great inspiration (see 1 Sam. 19:20-23).

The second level, the gift of prophecy, is also fairly common to today's Church. Unlike the spirit of prophecy, which falls upon whole congregations, this manifestation of prophecy is limited to a fewer number of people. As indicated in Chapter Four, it is one of the nine gifts of the Spirit found in First Corinthians 12 and is given by the Spirit "to whomever He wills." As mentioned, the gift of prophecy is a resident gift and can be utilized at any time by those who are developed in their gifting (see Acts 21:8-11).

The third level speaks of a prophetic mantle. It is a ministry function empowered by a strong prophetic anointing that rests upon an individual at all times. It far exceeds the first two levels in commitment and calling. In commitment, it requires a lifestyle devoted to the prophetic. In calling, it is often times preparatory for those who will later function as mature prophets. Much like Elisha, who received the mantle of the prophet Elijah, this prophetic mantle can fall upon a person who is in close association with a prophet or group of prophets (see 1 Kings 19:19; 2 Kings 2:15).

The fourth level embodies the office of a prophet. It is the highest realm of the prophetic. To possess this office, one is required to have a sovereign calling, extensive training, and multiple encounters with the Presence of God. Unlike the other levels of the prophetic, the prophet operates in a governmental office, directing and correcting the Church. He lives in a realm of forth-telling, rebuke, affirmation, revelation, illumination, divine utterance, prediction, encouragement, dreams, visions, exhortation, correction, and ministry confirmation (see Eph. 2:20; 4:11-12; 1 Cor. 12:28).

In summary, several points concerning these four levels of prophetic ministry must be clarified. First, any Christian can prophesy with an anointing at level one when the spirit of prophecy falls on a congregation. Next, levels one, two, and three are strictly for the encouragement, edification, and exhortation of the Church. Furthermore, the gift of prophecy at level two and the prophetic mantle at level three can be utilized by other ministries such as apostles, pastors, teachers, and evangelists. Finally, the fact that you operate with a gift of prophecy at level two, doesn't make you a prophet at level four. Only the level four office of a prophet has the latitude and the authority to direct and correct the Body of Christ.

Relating to Authority

When Jesus was asked to come and heal the servant of a certain centurion, the centurion said to Jesus:

> *...Just speak a word from where You are, and my servant boy will be healed! I know, because I am under the authority of my superior officers, and I have authority over my men. I only need to say "Go!" and they go....So just say, "Be healed!" and my servant will be well again!* (Luke 7:7-8 TLB)

 **When you are responsible for someone, you must also be responsible to someone. Thus, to have authority, you must also be under authority.**

When you are responsible *for* someone, you must also be responsible *to* someone. Thus, to have authority, you must also be under authority. The same applies to any person or ministry in today's Church. Whether a believer is pastor or prophet, church secretary or worship leader, all who labor in the Lord must defer to a higher authority than themselves. This act of submission places a believer in a flow of divine order.

Although many Christians wrestle with the issue of submission, God's order of authority is clear. First, we must submit to God. Next, we must submit to those whom God has placed over us. Finally, we must show an attitude of submission toward our peers. Scripture describes this as "submitting yourselves one to another in the fear of God" (Eph. 5:21).

Prophets and Submission

This brings up the issue of prophets submitting to authority. Have divinely called prophets erred in the areas of authority and submission? And, if so, is there a safeguard against them falling into what some would describe as a "spirit of independence"?

John Donne said, "No man is an island, entire of itself." If we believe this is true, then all Christians are part of the larger picture. For those who are prophetic, this bigger picture is the local church. In the same way that the New Testament prophets were church-based, prophetic people must also be accountable to the authority structure God has established. Without this connection we are in danger of becoming isolated Lone Rangers, and will act like renegade prophets who answer to none but ourselves. This applies to all levels of prophetic ministry (see Acts 13:2; 15:22).

In the last few years, the words *submission* and *authority* have become nasty language for most believers. With the prophetic there is even greater contention over whom the prophet should submit to, if anyone. A number of Christians believe the prophet is autonomous and answers to no one but God. Some say that the prophet must be under the authority of a seasoned apostle. Others declare that the prophet's ministry is subordinate to the pastor of the church where he attends or ministers. (Note: I'm not referring to those who are just prophetic or who have the gift of prophecy, but solely to those who function in the office of prophet.)

Which of these opinions is correct? Are there instances where all these concepts apply? Perhaps, but because the emphasis of this chapter concerns the breach between prophet and pastor, I will only comment on the issue of submission to the pastor. In my opinion, the prophet, himself, is not under any scriptural obligation to subject his ministry to pastors in general. Other than submitting to the pastor whom he frequently relates to (such as the pastor of the church where he is based or a pastor to whom he is connected in a covenant relationship), he is free to conduct his life under the guidance of the Holy Spirit.

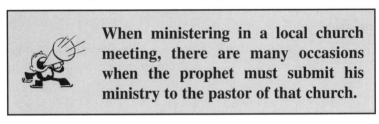

When ministering in a local church meeting, there are many occasions when the prophet must submit his ministry to the pastor of that church.

On the other hand, when ministering in a local church setting, the prophet must submit his ministry to the pastor of that church. From the time he enters the church meeting until he leaves, the prophet must be sensitive to the pastor's authority over that congregation. Unless the pastor fully releases his governmental rights to the prophet, the prophet is limited in doing only that which is allowed by the pastor. If the prophet attempts to minister contrary to the limitations set by the pastor, he is in direct violation of spiritual authority.

Therefore, the prophet has three choices. He can choose to submit himself to the wishes of that particular pastor. He can go to another church where he is fully accepted and released to minister. Or, he can conduct his meetings in a place other than a local church.

The Pastor's Role

Now I want to speak, by way of analogy, to prophets who might not understand a pastor's right of authority in his own church. In my opinion, the position that a pastor holds in his church is much like the position held by the head of a household. Both have the authority to regulate, establish protocol, set boundaries, etc. In respect to this principle, which of you would enter a man's house and attempt to do as you please? None, I'm sure. If the head of the house requested that you take off your shoes before entering, then out of respect, you would comply. If he said dinner would be served at five o'clock, then you would come to the table at five, not six. The rules might seem unnecessary or even silly, but, nonetheless, they are the rules of that house. Right or wrong, he is the head of his home and deserves respect from those who enter into his sphere of influence.

 It is always better to submit to godly authority than to undermine authority.

The same is true of a church and its pastor. While in his sanctuary, you come under his authority. If the pastor doesn't want you to lay hands on people, then don't lay hands on people. When he restricts you from prophesying, then don't prophesy. If he gives you 30 minutes to speak, then take 30, not 40. Remember, it's always better to submit to godly authority than to undermine authority.

Finally, if you feel that as a prophet you cannot comply with the rules, then don't hang around to complain or cause trouble. Instead, go privately to the pastor and kindly inform him that under the present circumstances you're unable to return and minister prophetically in his church. Then ask God to lead you to a church that is more compatible with your ministry. Pray that you will be hooked up with a pastor who understands your prophetic ministry and is sympathetic to your methods, doctrine, and ministry style.

The same principles apply to those who have a prophetic gift or prophetic mantle. If your church doesn't encourage prophetic ministry, don't push the issue. Either stay and pray that God will change things, or speak with the pastor and ask his blessing to find another church more favorable to the prophetic. Whatever the decision, remember to keep a good attitude.

A Prophet's *Metron*

> *But we will not boast of things without our measure, but according to the measure of the rule which God hath distributed to us....For we stretch not ourselves beyond our measure...* (2 Corinthians 10:13-14).

Metron is the Greek word for "measure." It means "portion or degree." In this instance of Scripture, it refers to the apostle's rule, but it can also be applied to a prophet's degree of rule, domain, or authority. In any case, the word *metron* can be used in a positive sense to reveal the measure of one's authority. In a negative sense, it can also reveal the limitations of that authority.

In the level four office of a prophet, there are two different *metrons* of a prophet's rule. One is *local rule*; the other is the *national/global rule*. A prophet who has been given local rule is one who has authority in a church or churches within his city. His realm of influence is limited to a local level. He works in concert with others to build up the city church. Since he is submitted to local eldership and rarely goes outside his area to minister, he is known by some as an in-house prophet.

The *national/global prophet* is called to the Church at large, and like the apostle Paul, he travels from city to city in an attempt to encourage and strengthen the corporate Body of Christ. His vision is broader; his authority is weightier; his anointing is usually different than that of the local prophet. He, too, is submitted to eldership. Nevertheless, he has more of a pioneering spirit, which enables him to move from region to region. His metron is only limited by an occasional restriction of the Holy Spirit, such as Paul experienced when he attempted to go into Asia (see Acts 16:4-6).

Out of Your *Metron*

Most contemporary prophets believe that their *metron* stretches as far as their airplane tickets. At times, this may be true for national/global prophets, but for local prophets it's dangerous to go where you haven't been called. Any attempt to minister in an area that you haven't been graced or equipped for can subject you to the attack of territorial spirits in that region. You could be hit with great temptation, physical and mental fatigue, depression, sickness, or even death (see 1 Kings 13).

Prophets must, therefore, determine how and where they will relate to the Church. If you are a local prophet, then stay home and support the pastors in your city. Give your attention to the building up of the local church. Focus on the needs around you, not the needs around the world. If you are a national/global prophet, then establish a network of relationships with elders of various regions. Make sure that you work in harmony with God's global purpose for the whole Body of Christ. Endeavor to excel in the edification of the whole Church instead of settling into the comfort zone of only one congregation.

Prophet/Pastor

A new breed of ministers is emerging in the 1990s. I call them *prophetic pastors*. It appears that in many situations God is placing prophets in a pastoral or associate pastor's position. This phenomenon may be short-lived, but for a time the Church will have to submit to it as an unprecedented work of the Holy Spirit.

Why would God allow a season when prophets pastor the Church? The answer is threefold. First, Jesus is still the Head of His Church and can make any adjustment He so desires. If He wishes to set a prophet in a church as pastor, who are we to say otherwise? (We don't seem to mind when an evangelist or teacher holds a pastoral position.) Furthermore, because supernatural ministry has been stifled by a number of traditional pastors, the Church is in need of a prophetic shot in the arm. To do this will take a concentrated effort from those who live and breathe the prophetic.

 Many insensitive and unloving prophets need to be dipped into the deep waters of pastoral responsibility.

Finally, but most importantly, many insensitive and unloving prophets need to be dipped into the deep waters of pastoral responsibility. They need to experience the incredible task of overseeing a church. They also need to be introduced to the never-ending chore of counseling floundering marriages, comforting those in distress, discerning the wolves, protecting the lambs, feeding the sheep, marrying the young, burying the dead, rebuking the disobedient, and encouraging the faithful. Moreover, they can benefit from the experience of being a spiritual father, mother, priest, teacher, midwife, policeman, and general problem-solver.

Give a prophet six months of pastoring, and I assure you he will have a different attitude toward pastors. The next time he enters a pastor's church, compassion and empathy will ooze out of him like honey from a honeycomb. Instead of doing his own thing, he will be inclined to accommodate the pastor in any way possible.

Part Three

Understanding Prophetic Failure and Success

Chapter Eleven

propHetic failure

The word *failure* has many negative connotations. For most people it means "to be insufficient, unsuccessful, to fall short, or to stop operating." It also implies that the person who fails does so because he is weak, faulty, imperfect, or immature. Therefore, no one aspires to be a failure.

Yet, in spite of our reluctance to admit it, failure is one of life's realities that must be reckoned with. Sooner or later failure knocks on everyone's door. When failure comes, we have several choices. We can attempt to ignore it, hide from it, run from it— or we can face failure head on and use it as a stepping-stone to success. Depending on your attitude, failure can either be a friend or an enemy. As an enemy, it can serve as a fatal end to your dreams—as a friend, it can become a launching pad to God's blessing in your life. Hence, you can serve failure, or failure can serve you. The choice is yours.

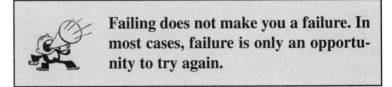

Failing does not make you a failure. In most cases, failure is only an opportunity to try again.

Failing does not make you a failure. In most cases, failure is only an opportunity to try again. This was the philosophy of a wise king named Solomon. In Proverbs 24:16 (NKJ), he wrote:

"For a *righteous* man may fall seven times and rise again...."
Notice, the Proverbs 24 man is called *righteous*, not because he
was without failure, but because he was willing to rise out of his
failure.

Many people who have succeeded in life began as failures.
This is true of many biblical characters. *Moses* delivered a whole
nation from bondage after he had failed miserably in a previous
attempt. *Rahab* was a harlot prior to helping the spies Joshua had
sent into Jericho. *David* became one of the most beloved kings of
all times in spite of moral failures such as adultery and murder.
Peter was given the commission to feed and care for the Church
shortly after he had denied Christ. And, *Paul*, who many acknowledge to be one of the greatest apostles of the New
Testament, was initially known for his zeal in killing Christians.

These are but a few of the biblical characters who refused to
be intimidated by their failures. After failing repeatedly, most of
them repented, arose from their despair, shook off the condemnation, and proceeded to be all that God had purposed for them
to be. They treated failure as a temporary setback, not as an
excuse to quit trying.

Fear of Failure

Three kinds of people travel the road to success: those who
fail and never try again, those who fail but keep on trying until
they succeed, and those who neither fail nor succeed because
they are afraid to try. Of the three, the latter is the worst. This person is crippled, not by failure, but by the fear of failure. He has
not learned that *"It is better to have tried and failed, than to fail
by not trying."*

The same is true of prophetic ministry today. I have seen
scores of Christians who desire to flow in the prophetic, but who
are afraid to try. An irrational fear of being wrong or making a
mistake has caused them to spend most of their lives dreaming
about prophecy rather than appropriating the prophetic gift within them. These Christians fail to prophesy, not for lack of desire,
but because they cling to an Old Testament mentality, which

demands that a prophet be stoned to death if he makes even the slightest error in his prophecy. Therefore, out of fear they refrain from speaking the word of the Lord.

Regardless of our fears, the beauty of New Testament Christianity is rooted in the concept that we are no longer under the judgment of Old Testament law. Unlike our Old Testament counterparts, who were often killed for their failures, we as contemporary Christians have been given New Testament grace to grow and mature through a process of trial and error. The writer of Hebrews 5:14 makes this clear by stating that mature Christians are those who have had their faculties trained by reason of use. The implication is that we, as New Testament believers, mature through a process of exercising and practicing our gifts.

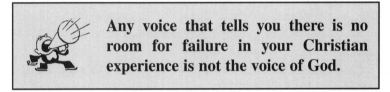

Any voice that tells you there is no room for failure in your Christian experience is not the voice of God.

Therefore, believers who desire to prophesy should remember four things. First, any voice that tells you there is no room for failure in your Christian experience is not the voice of God. Second, you will never succeed in God unless you are willing to fail in front of your peers. Third, instead of being crippled by the fear of failure, get up and try again and again until you get it right. Finally, when learning to prophesy by trial and error, you should limit your prophecy to the realm of edification, exhortation, and comfort. Remember, you cannot prophesy ministry confirmation, direction, and correction while utilizing the method of trial and error. A mistake in one of these categories of prophecy could be devastating to the person or to the church who receives your prophetic word.

Admitting Failure

Unlike the believers just described, a number of prophetic people have no fear of failure. Even so, when this particular group of Christians do fail, they are usually reluctant to admit it. It seems they will do almost anything to cover their misguided prophecies. They will lie, twist words, manipulate circumstances, and even attempt to blame God for their mistakes. When that doesn't work, the blame is then shifted to the person receiving the prophecy. The other person is told, "If you just had enough faith, my prophecy would have come to pass in your life."

A few years ago, I witnessed a classic case of prophetic failure that was compounded by denial. A prophet who was ministering to a young married couple prophesied that they would have a baby boy. Shortly afterward, the wife conceived and eventually gave birth. But, to the surprise of everyone, the baby was a girl. When confronted about his prophecy, the prophet replied, "Hey, if you would have had faith in my prophecy, the baby would have been a boy instead of a girl." It seemed the prophet wanted credit for prophesying the baby's birth, but was unwilling to admit that he had failed in predicting the gender.

Now there's nothing wrong with an honest mistake. Like the prophet in the example above, we have all missed it now and then. However, an honest mistake must be followed by an honest apology. What the prophet should have said was, "I sensed you were going to conceive a child but I failed to perceive the sex of your baby."

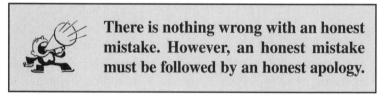

There is nothing wrong with an honest mistake. However, an honest mistake must be followed by an honest apology.

Had this man been honest, I believe God would have honored his integrity with a greater measure of prophetic anointing. Chances are, the next time he gave a prophecy, the results would have been more favorable. He needed to learn that *God resists the proud and gives grace to the humble* (see 1 Pet. 5:5).

When Prophecy Fails

Inaccurate prophecies occur for a number of reasons: inexperience, pride, or presumption on the behalf of the one who prophesies. These things greatly impact the purity of a prophetic word and are common to people who are immature. However, sometimes incorrect words are also given by seasoned prophets. For no apparent reason, these prophets seem to occasionally miss the mark, much like a gun that misfires periodically.

What is the reason for this inconsistency? Why do well-developed prophets give birth to prophetic duds now and then? Is there a safeguard against wayward prophecies? If so, what method can we employ to consistently deliver accurate prophecies? The answer lies in a threefold dynamic we will classify as "prophetic protocol." Many failed prophecies come from an error made in one of these three areas. Let me explain!

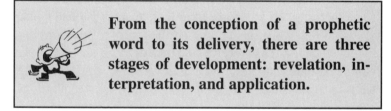

From the conception of a prophetic word to its delivery, there are three stages of development: revelation, interpretation, and application.

From the conception of a prophetic word to its delivery, there are three basic stages of development: revelation, interpretation, and application. All three are connected in sequential order and must be applied in the same manner. If you isolate one of these stages from the other in an attempt to shortcut prophetic procedure, the result could be devastating. Therefore, gaining an understanding of these stages and the way they are handled is fundamental to the success of any prophecy. For this reason, we will examine this procedure in the following pages and attempt to explain how it relates to the success or failure of prophecy.

Revelation

Revelation is the first stage in the development of a prophecy. This is where initial contact is made with the spirit world and prophetic information is obtained. This information is most commonly known as a *Rhema word* or *specific revelation*. As previously indicated, the information can come in many different forms—such as dreams, visions, inner-quickening, and inner-voice.

However, the problem of receiving revelation in any form is discerning its origin. This is where undeveloped and immature prophets are prone to make errors in judgment. Their sensitivity and openness to revelatory communication causes them to be, at times, subject to input from sources other than God's Spirit, sources such as the spirit of man, human imagination, soulish impressions, or even familiar spirits.

For instance, the prophetic person has an unusual receptivity heightening his or her capacity to receive revelation from God. However, this revelation is sometimes mixed with information from other sources. Much like a car radio that occasionally picks up two different stations on one channel, people who have not fine-tuned their gift can receive a mixture of information. For that reason, extreme caution must be used when receiving revelation that is to be translated into prophecy. We must ask the questions: *Is it wholly God? Is it the result of an overactive imagination? Is it input from a familiar spirit? Or, is it a mixture of one or more of these things?*

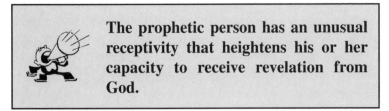

The prophetic person has an unusual receptivity that heightens his or her capacity to receive revelation from God.

When I was a young man, I had an experience that is typical of discerning the origin of revelation. While thinking about a particular member of my family, I saw a mental picture of what appeared to be an angel. This supposed *holy angel* began to speak to me about a family member. In a near audible voice, he said, "Your relative is going to fall sick and die within three days." As quick as the mental vision came, it also disappeared.

Although I did not doubt the reality of this visitation, I was left with the difficult task of discerning its source. *Was it from God or was it from an alternate source?* As I began to pray about the matter, I felt an inner witness that the revelation was not from God. It seemed that I was to consider the visitation as a powerless threat from a demonic *angel of light.*

Three days passed, and much to my relief the revelation had proven to be inaccurate (as I had anticipated). In fact, 15 years have passed, and the person who was supposed to die is still living. For the sake of all parties involved, I'm glad I was able to properly discern the revelation. Had I spoken this word as a prophetic utterance, the error would have unnecessarily frightened my family and jeopardized the integrity of my prophetic ministry.

Interpretation

Interpretation is the second stage in the development of prophecy. After you have determined that the source of your revelation is God, you must interpret its meaning. This step in your procedure cannot be ignored. Proper interpretation of your prophecy is just as important as discerning the origin. Therefore, before speaking a revelation, we must ask ourselves the following questions: *How does the revelation apply to the person I am ministering to? Can I give an interpretation that is relevant to his or her situation? Do I interpret my revelation at face value, or is it a coded or cryptic message that has several different meanings?* These questions are especially important for the prophetic person whose revelation comes in symbolic form.

For instance, if you see a vision of a candle over someone's head, how would you interpret this? Does it mean the person works at a candle factory, that he is the light of Christ, or that it's his birthday? If you have an impression that someone has no shoes, what does it mean? Does God want that person to be blessed with a new pair of shoes, are her feet ready to be "shod with the gospel of peace," or is she standing on holy ground like Moses at the burning bush?

This is where many prophetic people miss it. In the previous examples, any one of the interpretations could have applied. The proper interpretation could depend upon the circumstances related to the individual and, most importantly, to the specific purpose of God for that person. Therefore, to make accurate interpretations, we need to exercise patience and common sense. We also need a great measure of God's grace.

I want to cite another example illustrating the necessity of coupling revelation with proper interpretation. One evening after a Bible study, I was asked to minister to a lady who was having severe emotional problems. We will call her Mary. Touched by Mary's plea for help, I immediately began to pray about her situation. Halfway through my prayer, I had a vision of a broom lying beside Mary. I was certain the revelation came from God, but I was unsure of the interpretation. In my mind I began to ask myself several questions.

I mused: *Did God want to sweep Mary's past away? Or, had she been abused by someone whose last name was Broom? Was her occupation housecleaning or did the broom represent witchcraft in her family line?* I wasn't sure.

Eventually, after more prayer the interpretation became clear to me. As a small girl, Mary had become angry with her brother and had broken a broom across his back, severely injuring him. After the incident they were separated, and she was never able to ask his forgiveness. As a result, Mary had gone through life not forgiving herself for her violent act.

When the correct interpretation of this *Rhema* word was given to Mary, she broke down and began to weep uncontrollably. Indeed, it was true. This suppressed memory of the past was the root of her emotional problem. After recognizing it, she was immediately freed from a life of emotional imprisonment caused by self-hatred. Mary was thankful for the prophetic word, but I was equally thankful for the proper interpretation. Had I given a hasty interpretation of Mary's word, she might have never received the deliverance she so desperately needed.

Application

Application is the final stage in the development of a prophecy. After discerning the source of your revelation and interpreting it correctly, you must then know how to apply it. *Should it be given privately to the individual or publicly for all to hear? Should it be presented in the form of poetic prophecy, exhortation, or prophetic counseling? Should your approach be straightforward or diplomatic? And, most importantly, do you present your revelation with grace, judgment, soberness, or humor?* These are some of the questions facing the person who desires to successfully deliver a prophetic word.

Without close consideration of these questions, most people will experience undesirable results in the application of their prophecy. I have witnessed this breakdown in prophetic protocol over and over again. In fact, I have encountered scores of Christians who rightly receive and interpret revelation, but fail to apply it correctly.

Several years ago I was in a meeting where a prophetic person singled out a young man and began to minister to him. He said, "I see a vision of a black stain on your heart, and I interpret that as sin in your life." He then proceeded to expose the young man's sins publicly, calling him to repentance.

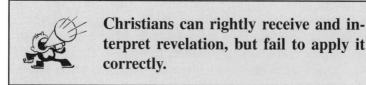

Christians can rightly receive and interpret revelation, but fail to apply it correctly.

The prophecy appeared to be an accurate word from God. However, because I knew the young man's history, I rejected the word on the basis of incorrect application. It's true—there had been moral failure in the man's life, but I knew that he had fully repented many years ago. In my opinion, the revelation of the dark stain and its interpretation was accurate but the application was dead wrong. What the young man needed was a reminder that God had already forgiven him, not another call to repentance.

He needed encouragement and affirmation of God's love, not fresh condemnation and guilt from an immature prophet.

Like the prophetic person in this illustration, we have all received a valid revelation now and then. Yet, the fact that we see things relating to people's lives does not mean that we have the correct interpretation or application for that revelation. For this reason, we must strive to minimize our failures by growing in our understanding of the three stages of prophetic protocol: revelation, interpretation, and application. Proper emphasis in these areas by those prophesying would greatly diminish our chances of delivering a faulty prophecy.

Conditional Prophecy

In addition to human error in the process of revelation, interpretation, and application, there is yet another twofold reason for failed prophecies. The first component relates to the will of man. The second has to do with the conditions set forth by God for a prophecy. In view of these facts, we must ask the following questions: *Does man's will contribute to the success or failure of a prophecy? Will God cause a prophetic word we have personally received to come to pass without our consent? Are there spoken prophecies that never materialize because certain conditions aren't met?*

Before answering these questions, we must first determine the latitude of man's will. To begin, the Bible supports two basic truths. First, man has been given considerable freedom to exercise his will. Since he possesses this freedom of choice, his will is not subject to the demands of Heaven or hell. He, alone, has the sole right of decision making and can utilize it for good or bad, right or wrong. Next, God does not arbitrarily violate a person's will to achieve His purpose in his or her life. The Almighty has chosen to work within the boundaries of human will, which often limits Him to the consent of mankind. Therefore, when God has a purpose for a man and expresses it through prophecy, the man's will must also be submitted to that prophetic purpose.

Therefore, both the success and failure of a prophetic utterance is contingent upon the spiritual posture of the person receiving the word. The person either complies with that word, denies its power, or worse, incurs judgment by disobeying the word that is given. Based on this premise, all prophecy is conditional.

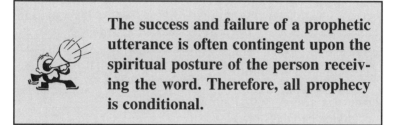

The success and failure of a prophetic utterance is often contingent upon the spiritual posture of the person receiving the word. Therefore, all prophecy is conditional.

This principle is clearly illustrated in the Book of Exodus. Initially, God spoke the prophetic word to Pharaoh, "Let My people go!" Pharaoh hardened his heart and, as a result, incurred God's judgment upon Egypt and its land, waters, buildings, produce, livestock, and people. God also spoke a prophetic word to Israel declaring that the people would leave Egypt and enter a land of promise called Canaan. Instead of receiving that word and being obedient to it, Israel received the evil report that "there were giants in the land and we were grasshoppers in their sight" (see Num. 13:33). The generation who had been delivered from bondage in Egypt became bound by their fears. By being disobedient to God, they incurred His wrath and died in the wilderness, never reaching their destination.

Who was to blame? Was the word that they received a true word from God? Indeed it was! God had fully revealed His intentions for Israel through the prophet Moses. Nevertheless, the children of Israel were reluctant to align their wills with the prophetic word spoken to them. Since they had set themselves against God by grumbling, complaining, and walking in unbelief, the Word of God was made null and void in their lives. As a result, the promise was passed to the next generation. Those to whom the promise was given died without ever receiving it. At the same time, their offspring became the beneficiaries of a prophetic word that was not initially spoken to them.

Elsewhere in the Bible, we see this same principle working in reverse fashion. According to the Book of Jonah, God had purposed the destruction of a city called Nineveh and instructed Jonah the prophet to declare this imminent judgment. Yet, after hearing the prophetic word of God, the citizens of that city humbled themselves and repented. As a result, the word spoken by the prophet didn't come to pass. Obviously, Jonah was not happy with his failed prophecy, but he learned that prophecy is conditional, depending upon the posture of man's will.

Overview of Prophetic Failure

In view of God's grace, we should never let the fear of failure neutralize our prophetic gift. When we fail, we need to get up and try again and again until we get it right. Remember, we will not be judged for making an honest mistake. God sees us as children and makes allowances for our growth and development. Also remember that the trial and error method does not apply to directional or correctional prophecy. It only applies to basic prophetic ministry such as edification, exhortation, and comfort.

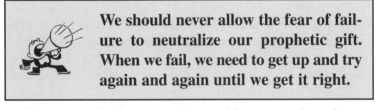

We should never allow the fear of failure to neutralize our prophetic gift. When we fail, we need to get up and try again and again until we get it right.

Next, as we begin to grow in our gift, we must learn how to minimize our mistakes. When we receive prophetic insight from God, we must be sure that we have the right interpretation and application for that word before we deliver it. This will increase our accuracy and bring greater credibility to our ministry.

Finally, be aware that prophecy is conditional. Since man's will is involved, some prophetic words will never come to pass. For this reason, when giving or receiving a prophecy, be aware that the success of that prophecy most likely depends upon the person's compliance with the Spirit of God. Remember, *we cannot turn our backs on God nor set our wills against His purpose and expect a prophetic word to blossom in our lives.*

Chapter Twelve

prophetic pitfalls

In the English language, *pitfall* is defined as "a lightly covered hole in the ground, designed to entrap unwary prey." In a broader sense, *pitfall* speaks of any kind of hidden danger. When Paul writes about the "snare of the devil" in Second Timothy 2:26, the Greek word *pagis* is used, meaning "a trap that is set." Therefore, in both secular and biblical language, pitfalls are places of entrapment that should be avoided at all cost.

The old gospel road is filled with dangerous pitfalls. At every turn there are opportunities to fall prey to the snares of the devil. Many who walk circumspectly will avoid these snares; others who are ignorant of satan's traps will be taken captive. The choice is ours; we can stumble in the darkness or allow the Lord to be "a lamp unto our feet, and a light unto our path" (see Ps. 119:105).

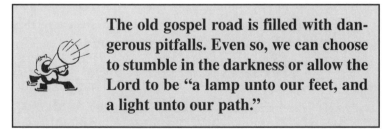

The old gospel road is filled with dangerous pitfalls. Even so, we can choose to stumble in the darkness or allow the Lord to be "a lamp unto our feet, and a light unto our path."

What are some of these snares in relation to the prophetic? How do they damage those who prophesy? How do they limit the effectiveness of prophetic people? And, once we understand the potential pitfalls of the prophetic, what action can we take to avoid them?

"Thus Saith the Lord"

In today's Church a "God told me" mentality seems to dominate the thinking of many believers. Just ask Christians their opinion on something, and usually you will get a "God told me" or "The Lord showed me" response. It seems that God speaks to those believers hundreds of times a day, about hundreds of different things. Everything from doctrinal issues to world events fall under the umbrella of "Thus saith the Lord."

Young Christians have also learned to use these magic words to their own advantage. When their opinions are contradicted by spiritual truth or biblical logic, they will often resort to the same old "God told me so" tactic. If you continue to press them, they will eventually jump the fence of reasoning with a statement like, "Hey, all I know is what God has revealed to me!" Since one is hard-pressed to argue with a believer who hides behind a "Thus saith the Lord," from that moment on all effective, two-way conversation is concluded.

Prophetic people contend with a similar temptation. They, too, are tempted to declare, "Thus saith the Lord," in most situations. This is especially true of undeveloped prophets who feel under pressure to come up with a word from God. As a result of peer pressure, they often confuse God's voice with their own opinions. Driven by impatience, many of these immature prophets often speak what God has not said. Consequently, they give prophetic assumptions rather than divine guidance.

Driven by impatience, immature prophets often speak what God has not spoken. As a result, they give prophetic assumptions rather than divine guidance.

Many people learn the lesson of presumption the hard way. With me, it began some years ago when I was conducting a prophetic conference on the West Coast. While in the process of ministering to a group of people, I turned to a lady and boldly declared, "Thus saith the Lord." Before I could finish my prophecy, I was interrupted by the voice of God who whispered these words to my spirit: "I am not speaking to this lady right now. You are on your own." He further indicated that I could speak for myself, but I could not use His name to make my point.

I immediately corrected myself and said to her, "Thus saith Larry." Assuming that I was making a joke, everyone began to laugh at my statement. I, too, paused and chuckled for a moment. Then, to the surprise of those in the room, I proceeded to speak prophetically into the lady's life. I'm not sure how well it was received. However, in my mind I was taking the approach that Paul used when he said to the Corinthian church: "I say this, as my own word, not as the Lord's." He went on to say that his opinions on the issues addressed were most likely the same as the Lord's. "That is my opinion," he said, "and I believe that I too have the Spirit of God" (see 1 Cor. 7:12,40 NEB).

It's important to note the following: In these Scriptures the apostle seemed to be saying, "Thus saith Paul." In my opinion, he was not attempting to play God but was simply taking the liberty to express his own thoughts, as one who possessed the mind of Christ. I'm sure Paul's words were true, inspired, and packed with godly wisdom, but at the same time, he wasn't comfortable in declaring it as a *"Thus saith the Lord"* statement.

In the same way, unless you are certain that God is speaking directly into a situation, it would be better to leave His name out of most prophecies. It would be safer to say, "I think, I feel, I sense, I perceive, I discern," than to box yourself into a corner with a "Thus saith God." Furthermore, if you have an opinion about something, then call it an opinion or a prophetic opinion if you will, but by no means should you call it *the word of God.*

If you involve God in something He has not initiated, the consequences could be severe. You could be judged according to the

Scripture found in Deuteronomy 18:22 (RSV): "When a prophet speaks in the name of the Lord, if the word does not come to pass or come true, that is a word which the Lord has not spoken; the prophet has spoken it presumptuously...." If you fail this test, you could be labeled as a false prophet.

King James Vernacular?

While in Mexico, I once heard an amusing tale that was very thought-provoking. A Englishman and a Mexican were riding together in a car, arguing about the color of God. The white man insisted that God was white; the Mexican was convinced God was brown. Suddenly, the car ran off the road, killing both men. Moments later they awoke in Heaven in front of the Pearly Gates. As they approached God's throne, the white man began to shout with excitement. Pointing at the Great White Throne, he yelled, "See, I told you God was white just like me." About this time, the Lord leaned over and said to both of them, "Hola muchachos, bienvenidos" (Spanish for "Hello, friends, come on in").

Like those men in the story, we, too, think that God looks and speaks the same way we do. Nevertheless, God, who is a Spirit, is neither white, brown, black, red, nor green; nor is He bound to any one form of communication. He chooses to speak to people in their own language, not because He prefers one language over another, but for the sake of their understanding.

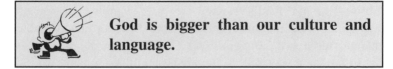

God is bigger than our culture and language.

God is bigger than our culture and language. For this reason, we should never limit the Almighty to a particular people, group, or dialect. This truth is especially important for the Christian who is a devoted fan of the King James Bible. Those who live, breathe, and quote this translation should be aware that the King James Version is only one of the many translations taken from the original Greek and Hebrew Scriptures. Therefore, when preaching or prophesying, you are not being unspiritual or unscriptural to omit some of the *yea, nay, thus,* and *thou* words characteristic of sixteenth century English (King James language). In fact, people will be more inclined to hear your message if they are addressed in a language familiar to their ears.

I know that I'm treading on the sacred ground of many believers. I'm also aware that I run the risk of being labeled a heretic. Nonetheless, those who are dogmatic about prophesying or preaching exclusively in King James vernacular should consider several issues.

First, the Word of God didn't originate in merry old England, and Jesus didn't speak the King's English while on earth. He was born in the Middle East some 1,600 years before the King James Bible was ever envisioned. He was also Jewish and spoke in an Arabic tongue. So, by all means read, study, memorize, and cherish the King James translation, but please don't try to convince yourself or others that it is the ultimate translation or that you must use it to get the proper results.

Second, we must try to break the King James stereotype, which is common to most prophetic people. I am not suggesting that we discard the King James Bible, but when possible we should read other translations and commit the passages to memory. As a result of this diversity, our preaching style and prophetic delivery might become richer and less constrained. Remember, if it is God's Word, then it can survive a diversity of translations.

If it is God's Word, then it can survive a diversity of translations.

Finally, if we serve a God who is bigger than language, then we, too, must not be narrow-minded in our communication. For instance, the next time you are tempted to prophesy, "Thus saith the Lord God Almighty, thou art extolled by Him that sitteth upon the circle of the earth," try to restrain yourself. Instead, say something like, "Hey, I really think that God loves you!"

Screamers

Many prophetic people have a tendency to prophesy with a loud voice. With the energy of a cattle-yard auctioneer, they yell, scream, and holler at their audience. The longer they speak, the louder they get, until someone responds by buying what they are selling. The result is usually a hand clap from the audience, a cheer, or a barrage of "amens."

This is especially true of many Pentecostals and Charismatics. There is a basic belief that the anointing is equivalent to noise. The theory is: The louder the volume, the greater the power. They believe that by shaking the walls of the church with a high-decibel prophecy, God will come through with greater impact. On rare occasions this may be true, but usually screaming is nothing more than a frantic attempt to compensate for inward fears, insecurities, and a lack of authority.

In my opinion, there is a time to be forceful, and a time to be gentle and soft. The proper approach depends on the dynamics of the situation at the time of the prophecy. If you need to lift your voice to be heard in a large room or auditorium, then by all means speak forcefully. Or if there is a need to penetrate a dull, sleepy, atmosphere with volume, then that, too, can be in order. In most cases, however, it is not appropriate to yell in people's faces. This sort of behavior is rude and can be an insult to the intelligence of those who are receiving your ministry. For that reason, the next time you feel compelled to scream a prophecy in church, be aware...most Christians are not deaf!

Remember, if God does not yell or scream at His people, neither should we. It's true the prophets of old often cried out with a loud voice. Yet they yelled, not because it was the religious thing to do, but because they were addressing masses of people without the aid of a public address system. Therefore, when you prophesy, find a microphone and speak to the congregation in a normal tone of voice. I assure you it will not hinder the anointing. It is "not by might, nor by power, but by My spirit, saith the Lord" (Zech. 4:6).

God's Word or Human Disposition?

They angered him [Moses] *at the waters of Meribah, and it went ill with Moses on their account; for they made his spirit bitter, and he spoke words that were rash* (Psalm 106:32-33 RSV).

We have been called to express God's attitude, not human mood and temperament. Moses learned this lesson the hard way. While in the desert he was told by God to strike a rock with one blow, thus creating a miraculous flow of water. Instead, he became angry with the murmuring crowd of thirsty Israelites and smote the rock twice. Moses misrepresented the heart of God by displaying an improper attitude. As a result, he fell under divine judgment.

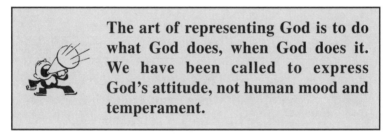

The art of representing God is to do what God does, when God does it. We have been called to express God's attitude, not human mood and temperament.

Like Moses, it's very common for today's prophets to speak out of their own disposition. Many understand the dangers of misrepresenting God, but all too often anger, strife, and bitterness seem to affect the purity of their prophetic word. If they have had a recent fight with their spouse, you can rest assured the Church will receive a scathing rebuke. If they are feeling melancholy, a disheartening prophecy will also surface. On the other hand, when they are experiencing a season of inner joy, the Church is bound to hear about the goodness and mercy of God.

The art of representing God is to do what God does, when God does it. Prophetic people must be willing to cry when God is crying and laugh when God is laughing. However, like Moses, most of us have it backward. We often smile when God is crying or cry when God is laughing. We have not learned to lay aside our emotions long enough to express the disposition of God. As a result, the Church doesn't know whether to repent or rejoice.

Recently, I was in a meeting where someone stood up and prophesied, "Thus saith the Lord, God hates your guts." Immediately, half of the people in the building bowed their heads to repent of whatever it was that made God so mad. As I looked at the person prophesying, I began to chuckle inside. I did not intend to receive such a prophecy. To begin with, I knew that God loves His children and would never say such a thing. Next, I discerned that the person prophesying had been harboring bitterness toward other Christians. And, finally, in my estimation the prophecy had come from *hurt*, not from *Heaven*. With these things in mind, I finally bowed my head and thanked God that His word is not subject to human mood.

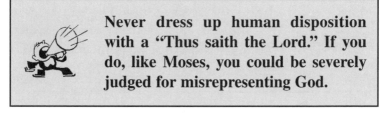

Never dress up human disposition with a "Thus saith the Lord." If you do, like Moses, you could be severely judged for misrepresenting God.

This incident, and others like it, has taught me two great truths. First, before you speak for God, make sure that your heart is a reflection of God's heart. And last, never dress up human disposition with a "Thus saith the Lord." If you do, like Moses, you could be severely judged for misrepresenting God.

Marriages and Babies?

There are instances in the Bible where marriages were consummated as a direct result of prophetic words (see Gen. 24:40; Hos. 1:1-2; Mt. 1:20). In addition to marriages, Scripture details several instances where children were born as the result of prophetic prediction. Occasionally their names and genders were also given before conception (see Judg. 13:3; Lk. 1:13,31).

In no instance of Scripture—other than Isaiah's prophecy concerning the birth of Jesus and John the Baptist—are babies and marriages predicted by prophets.

However, most predictions concerning marriages and babies in the Bible were the result of God speaking directly to those involved or by angelic visitation. In the cases of Samson, John, and Jesus, it was an angel that prophesied their births. In other Scripture relating to marriages, those involved received a personalized word directly from God's Spirit. Nevertheless, in no instance of Scripture—other than Isaiah's prophecy concerning the birth of Jesus and John the Baptist—are babies and marriages predicted by prophets.

In spite of the lack of biblical support for prophesying marriages and babies, many prophetic people still continue to venture into this area of prophecy. In certain cases, the results have been devastating. Barren women who have received prophetic words of hope from "marriage and baby prophets" often slip into deep depression after failing to conceive. In other instances, infants foretold to be boys turn out to be girls, and vice versa. Most commonly, marriages consummated as a result of so-called "prophetic words" are often shipwrecked after years of struggling with relationships that were never meant to be.

These horror stories are a sad testimony to the dangers of overstepping scriptural guidelines. If the Bible is our text for prophetic protocol, then we, as a prophetic people, must conduct our ministries in a way that is consistent with the patterns found in Scripture. If the Bible speaks out on certain issues, then we, too, can speak with confidence. If the Bible is silent on an issue, then we must also exercise extreme caution. We must take into consideration that things documented and repeated in Scripture must be of importance. Also, things scarcely mentioned in Scripture may be of lesser significance.

Such is the case of prophesies concerning babies and marriages. Although it is not out of the question to give such prophecies, this type of word should be more of an exception than a rule. In my opinion, the ratio should be something like one baby or marriage prophecy for every hundred prophecies of a different nature. Also, when these prophecies are given, they must be delivered with confidence and accuracy by mature and capable prophets—not with the hit-and-miss tactics practiced by a number of prophetic ministries.

Immature prophets who have overextended themselves in this area of prophecy need to be reminded of several things. First, their presumption exposes them to the danger of operating in the realm of soul power and soothsaying. Next, there is a fine line between the divine and divination, and without the check and balance of Scripture anyone is capable of crossing this critical line.

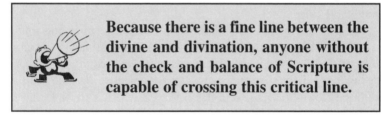

Because there is a fine line between the divine and divination, anyone without the check and balance of Scripture is capable of crossing this critical line.

Last, I have prophesied over barren women and have seen God honor the prophetic word with the miracle of childbirth. At times, I have been able to pinpoint the gender and exact date of delivery. Nevertheless, because of recent dealings in my ministry, I am attempting to restrain myself in this area of prophecy. For the sake of scriptural purity and prophetic balance, I am increasingly reluctant to venture into any gray areas of prophecy, especially of babies and marriage.

Money

One of the most common pitfalls for ministers today is the issue of money. Predicting great wealth for others or prophesying with the motive of personal gain can be alluring snares of the devil. For those who maintain a level of prophetic integrity, this may not be much of an issue. Yet, like Balaam of the Old Testament, many latter-day prophets have become *prophets for profit*. In other words, they are prophets to the Church only if it profits them first (see Jude 11).

In many instances, high-dollar prophets have cheapened their ministries with unholy tactics (selling their gifts for gain). While some of these prophets blatantly beg for money, others peddle tons of religious paraphernalia and gospel trinkets. Almost everything—from 1-800-Dial-a-Prophet phone service, to $100 prophecy lines, holy water, healing oils, and anointed clothes—have been marketed and sold under the guise of advancing the Kingdom of God.

In my opinion, this sort of nonsense has diminished the value of the prophetic. And, in due time, those who have merchandised themselves and their gifts in this fashion will be exposed. They will be marked by God as having "...forsaken the right way, and are gone astray, following the way of Balaam the son of Bosor, who loved the wages of unrighteousness" (2 Pet. 2:15).

The Bible clearly teaches that "the laborer is worthy of his reward." It is also true that "those who minister should be counted worthy of double honor." (See First Timothy 5:17-18.) Yet, when there is a season of financial leanness, we should *never* resort to prophetic manipulation for money. In spite of our lack, we must possess the same kind of integrity that motivated Elisha the prophet to refuse excessive gifts from Naaman the Syrian. Elisha realized that God's free expression of love for Naaman, as evidenced by God healing him of leprosy, did not entitle the

---

The Word of the Lord is not for sale. Freely we have received; freely we should give. However, like Balaam of the Old Testament, many latter-day prophets today have become prophets for profit.

prophet to take advantage of the Syrian's great wealth (see 2 Kings 5:1-27).

Like the prophet Elisha, we too must declare that the Word of the Lord is not for sale. Freely we have received; freely we should give. Anything less is a direct violation of true spiritual ministry and will be met with the wrath of God's judgment. Just as Jesus overturned the tables of merchandise in the Temple and drove out the moneychangers, He shall also appear in His righteous wrath and judge those who would fleece His flock, today. With whip in hand, He will purge His Father's temple from the flea-market mentality of buying and selling the things of God. That which has become a "den of thieves" will be cleansed and restored to a house of prayer and free ministry. In which case, we, as ministers, should learn to give, expecting nothing in return. Like God's priest who served in the Old Testament Temple, we should seek no inheritance other than the richness of God's Spirit.

Please understand, I am not suggesting that prophetic ministries refuse honorariums and offerings for their labor. Neither am I saying that they should refuse love gifts from those whom they have encouraged in the Lord. What I am saying is that material gain cannot be a priority. *Money must never take precedence over ministry.* Neither should the lack of it dictate how much you minister, nor to whom you minister.

Prophetic Manipulation

Webster's Dictionary defines *manipulation* as follows: "to control the will or emotions of another person by exploiting feelings such as guilt or affection to one's own ends; shrewd or devious effort to manage or influence for one's own purposes; to appropriate or control by skilled use."

The most serious pitfall awaiting those who minister in the prophetic is the temptation to manipulate people and circumstances with the gift of prophecy. Prophetic people who are rich in emotion and abundantly gifted can readily arouse people's interests and stir their hearts. Their capacity to hear from God allows them to serve as powerful magnets, drawing to themselves those who thirst for a word from God. As a result, they quickly win accolades and favor, making it easy for them to manipulate most believers.

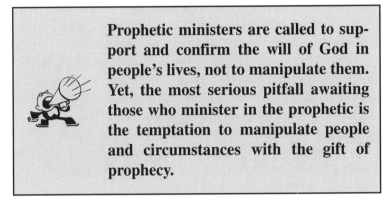

Prophetic ministers are called to support and confirm the will of God in people's lives, not to manipulate them. Yet, the most serious pitfall awaiting those who minister in the prophetic is the temptation to manipulate people and circumstances with the gift of prophecy.

This stands in direct opposition to the purpose of prophetic ministry. After all, prophetic ministers are called to support and confirm the will of God in people's lives, not to manipulate them. We are instructed in the Bible to encourage God's Church, not to control it.

In spite of this warning, I have observed ministries that have greatly abused the Church by manipulating God's people in three different areas. First, some prophets use their prophetic gifts to extort large sums of money from unsuspecting Christians. They often prophesy that, "God says give all to the prophet of God." Second, others use their giftedness and charisma to gain influence, manipulate leaders, and control circumstances favorable to their position. Finally, the most dangerous of all manipulators are those who influence the opposite sex to act in immoral and unbecoming ways.

Some of these ministers have prophesied that believers should divorce their marriage partners and find their true soul mates. Others have suggested that women become intimate with them as an act of servanthood, assuring them that it is all right to indulge in a lifestyle of promiscuity. Much like the prophet Balaam, they "cast a stumblingblock before the children of Israel," causing weak Christians to commit fornication (Rev. 2:14).

How do these prophetic ministries manage to gain such power over people's lives? To begin, their persuasive personalities serve as a hook to ensnare those of lesser maturity. Subsequently, because the essence of the prophetic revolves around the power of words, everything spoken by prophets has a dramatic impact on the hearers. Like a guided missile, the words of a prophet can seek out a target of weak conscience or guilt and explode deep within the soul of that person. Even those things spoken in jest or casual conversation can penetrate the most guarded heart and bring the person under the influence of the prophet's intentions. For this reason, prophets should exercise extreme caution in the manner they conduct their lives and ministries.

Prophets have the ability to either bless or curse with their mouths. Like a guided missile, the words of a prophet can seek out a target of weak conscience or guilt and explode deep within the soul of that person.

Finally, prophetic people should keep a guard on their mouths at all times. They must realize that every word spoken has the potential to wreak devastation. They must also understand that every word that leaves their mouths will take root and produce seed after its own kind—either good or bad. In this context, prophets have the ability to either bless or curse with their mouths. Jesus said,

And I will give unto thee the keys of the kingdom of heaven: and whatsoever thou shalt bind on earth shall be bound in heaven: and whatsoever thou shalt loose on earth shall be loosed in heaven (Matthew 16:19).

Counterfeits

That which God initiates, lucifer attempts to duplicate. This dynamic can be seen in every aspect of Christian experience. Any time a real work of the Holy Spirit takes place, rest assured that the devil will attempt to duplicate it with a counterfeit. This principle also applies to the prophetic.

For example, when the Holy Spirit imparts prophetic revelation to the Church, satan is also on hand, ready to inject a counterfeit anointing. This counterfeit gifting can come in many forms. It can surface as blatant satanism, white magic, palmistry, channeling, crystal healing, or it may appear as the seemingly harmless New Age movement.

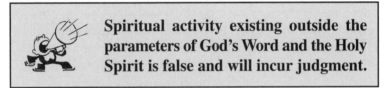

Spiritual activity existing outside the parameters of God's Word and the Holy Spirit is false and will incur judgment.

Those who are ignorant of satan's devices often fall prey to one or more of these pitfalls. They are unaware that spiritual activity existing outside the parameters of God's Word and the Holy Spirit is false and will incur judgment. This spiritual activity, absolutely forbidden by God in Scripture, is addressed in this manner: "There shall not be found among you any one...that useth divination, or an observer of times, or an enchanter, or a witch, or a charmer, or a consulter with familiar spirits, or a wizard, or a necromancer. For all that do these things are an abomination unto the Lord..." (Deut. 18:10-12).

A few years ago this truth was made real to me in a very personal way. I had been touring the nation, ministering in various churches and conferences. On one occasion I was in Phoenix, Arizona, conducting a prophetic conference for a group of churches. While en route to the meeting, I heard a familiar sound coming from a side room in the lobby. It seemed to be the voice of a man prophesying. Simultaneously, there was the sound of a weeping female (whom I assumed was the recipient of prophetic ministry). Apparently her cries were the result of a prophetic word relating to her past. She was given accurate information, such as dates and specific details concerning childhood trauma and then exhorted to release the past and move on with her life.

With great delight, I stepped out of the lobby and into the room, hoping to witness the ministry of the Holy Spirit. However, when I leaned over and peeked through the partially open door, I was stunned. Much to my surprise, I saw tables filled with crystals and chairs occupied by New Agers. It was apparent that I had stumbled onto a New Age seminar where the power of psychic perception was being demonstrated.

How can this be true? Has the world capitalized on counterfeit giftings, and are these people experiencing results? Undoubtedly, it appears that they not only possess a form of prophetic perception, but also excel in its use. Furthermore, these false ministers, such as television psychics and fortunetellers, are more than eager to demonstrate their psychic powers to a generation starving for a touch of the supernatural. Nevertheless, as spiritual as these things appear to be, we must remember that: *fortune-telling, seances, secret covens, Ouija boards, psychic phenomena, and New Age spiritualism are pitfalls that reek with the odor of false anointing and must be avoided at all cost.*

Chapter Thirteen

propHeTic weirDness

One of the most disturbing snares related to the prophetic is the exhibition of *weirdness*. The bizarre behavior and strange mannerisms of a number of prophetic people have caused the world to develop ideas about the prophetic, ideas that are incorrect. When the word *prophet* is mentioned, two distinct images appear within the minds of both sinner and saint. These images are *weird* and *bizarre*. Although the words *weird* and *bizarre* bear close resemblance, each group—sinners and saints—view them in a different manner, and for the most part both are wrong.

To most Christians, the stereotype of a prophet is one who is bizarre, archaic in thinking, crude in manners, and caustic in attitude. Prophets are seen as solitary hermits or cave dwellers who occasionally crawl out of their most holy habitations to rebuke a worldly Church. When they appear on the scene, a paralyzing fear strikes the hearts of both man and beast. Dogs begin to howl, babies cry, and women scramble for shelter, hiding their children from the wrath of these spiritual godzillas!

 One of the most disturbing snares related to the prophetic is the exhibition of weirdness.

As these giants ascend to the hallowed heights of the pulpit, hell and earth fall silent awaiting their commands. Everyone is breathless, knowing that a single move of the prophet's hand can topple empires, set churches in order, and expose the sins of carnal believers. No one is exempt; even demons flee from the lightning bolts issuing from the end of their long bony fingers. Although these prophets are called to the ministry of *equipping* the saints, they usually end up *whipping* the saints. Ruthlessly, they rip the hide off the backs of both sheep and shepherd and then pour salt into their open wounds.

Then, after thoroughly persecuting the saints, these prehistoric prophets mount their steeds, return to their Stone Age strongholds, and go into holy hibernation. Finally, after a season of strange visions and weird dreams, they rise once again, put on their camel-hair coats, eat a bowl of gun powder, pick their teeth with grasshopper legs, and prepare to minister again. *This is the picture most Christians have of the prophet and his ministry.*

In contrast, the world has quite a different perception of the prophetic. Instead of the medieval mentality held by the Church, the secular view of the prophetic is one of New Age imagery, much like the *Star Trek* movies. To them, a prophet is more of a "prophetic space cadet" than a normal man. He is a universal guru who has ascended to the spiritual heights of the third heaven. Going where no man has gone before, his intergalactic ministry reaches out to regions unknown, where he is able to communicate with spiritual entities of extraterrestrial origin.

This prophetic person is a type of New Age superman, able to leap tall buildings in a single bound. He flies by astro-projection, communicates with the dead, reads minds, and sees through the obscure. With the help of his crystal ball and the strength of his psychic powers, he sets the pace for a whole new breed of spiritualist. For this sort of space prophet, the Spirit of God is simply the force within. Satan is just an illusion from the dark side. Speaking in tongues is merely an eastern chant. Being slain in the Spirit means that he enters a state of bliss through transcendental meditation. Prophesying is a form of crystal gazing, and waiting on God means that the prophet is so spiritually advanced that he must stop and wait for the Almighty to catch up with him. *This seems to be the mind-set of the world concerning prophetic ministry.*

Both views, religious and worldly, serve only as reminders of the extreme misconceptions and myths that prophetic people face. Due to these false concepts, few people perceive prophetic ministry as being a normal, rational expression of Christian experience. Their negative perception of the prophetic is reinforced, not only by these myths, but also by prophets who conduct their ministries in a weird or unusual fashion.

Weird or Strange?

To the average observer there is little difference between *weird* and *strange.* Yet, to those who are alert and spiritually in tune, the two words are actually quite distinct. While *weird* denotes "being odd, queer, and bizarre"; the word *strange* is defined as "unusual, extraordinary, and peculiar." The first is closely akin to eccentric behavior, which is often unnatural and unacceptable. The latter word relates to uniqueness and is acceptable as a biblical expression.

I have encountered both weird and strange prophets. Although some of these prophets exhibit moderation, others seem to be much more *pathetic* than *prophetic.* At first, they may appear to be spiritual, but weird prophets are usually bizarre, spooky, and spiritually imbalanced. They profess to be pure as snow, but in most instances they can be more brainless than sinless. Driven by an ego larger than life, they humiliate not only themselves but also others who embrace their theatrical antics. May God save us from this kind of present-day weirdness!

Make no mistake—most prophetic people are seen as being a *strange* and *peculiar* people. Even so, that doesn't mean we have to act in a weird fashion. Like our biblical counterparts, we have the right to be unusual in our manner and method of ministry; however, we must also be "user-friendly"—able to relate to the Church and the world. We are certainly called to be different, but by no means are we called to be bizarre.

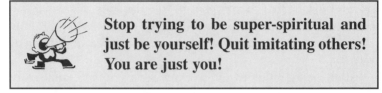

Stop trying to be super-spiritual and just be yourself! Quit imitating others! You are just you!

Therefore, I have a few things to say to weird Christians: *Knock it off! Stop trying to be super-spiritual and just be yourself! Quit imitating others!* You are not called to be another Elijah or John the Baptist, nor are you a prophetic parrot. You are just you! You are unique in personality, diverse in style, and different in expression. So, relax and *learn to be supernaturally natural.* Drop the weird stuff, and maybe God will entrust you with a legitimate ministry, one that is real and refreshing.

Bizarre Prophecies

One of the by-products of prophetic weirdness is bizarre prophecy. If a prophetic person is eccentric and unnatural, you can be assured that most of his or her prophecies are also off the wall. This person might be able to hide it for a while, but sooner or later the foolishness of his heart will be expressed in his actions and with his lips. "For out of the abundance of the heart his mouth speaks" (Lk. 6:45b RSV).

Over the years, I have witnessed much of the craziness generated by weird prophets and bizarre prophecies. I have seen a number of self-proclaimed seers who are convinced their weirdness comes from God. In obedience to the so-called *word of the Lord*, they have filled the gas tank of their stalled car with sugar, thrown rocks through the walls of the church sanctuary, handcuffed themselves to the pews of the church, and bound and gagged members of their congregation with duct tape.

Others have prophesied the end of the world within 24 hours, the instantaneous melting of snow on Mt. Ararat (which will supposedly reveal the location of Noah's Ark), and the formula for making hair spray. They have declared that the antichrist would emerge from the headquarters of the Democratic party, that the

Church would take over the world by military force, and that God was sick in bed, unable to perform His duties.

> One of the by-products of prophetic weirdness is bizarre prophecy. If a prophetic person is eccentric and unnatural, you can be certain that most of his or her prophecies are also off the wall.

In one meeting, a prophetic person stood up and said: "Thus saith the Lord God, 'I have seen your despair; yea, I know how you have suffered with your sickness; yea, I am also aware of your struggle with depression and suicidal thoughts; yea, I understand, for I, the Lord, went through the exact same thing last week.'" On another occasion someone prophesied the following: " 'Yea,' saith the Lord, 'I was going to speak to you but I forgot what I was going to say, so please pray for my memory,' saith the Lord." In another church, a lady stood up and declared, "Thus saith God, 'Just as Abraham parted the Red Sea, I shall also part your troubled waters.'" She sat down slowly, pondered the prophecy for a minute, stood up again and said, "Thus saith God, 'I have made a terrible mistake. It was not Abraham but Moses who parted the Red Sea.'"

Judging Weird Prophecies

Let the prophets speak two or three, and let the other judge (1 Corinthians 14:29).

Some of the crazy things said and done in the name of prophecy have made it necessary for believers to judge all things. Yet, other than the Bible and spiritual discernment, there seems to be no universal yardstick to use to systematically measure or judge prophecy. Therefore, in each instance when prophecy is given, we must take into consideration all the dynamics present at the time. When judging prophecies, we must make allowance for the mistakes of immature people. We need to extend grace and mercy to all prophetic words given by beginners and release them from any undue sense of condemnation or heavy-handed judgment. On the contrary, we must not be tolerant of the crazy and bizarre prophecies uttered by weird Christians.

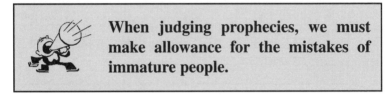

When judging prophecies, we must make allowance for the mistakes of immature people.

Are there times when weird prophecies are given by perfectly normal people? Absolutely! Yet, many times these prophecies are the result of fear, nervousness, or inexperience. Usually, they are innocent mistakes made through ignorance or a slip of the tongue. In light of this, it would be unwise to judge these people harshly or correct them publicly. All that is needed is a little backroom instruction and a lot of encouragement. With proper training these Christians can be groomed to operate in a clear, concise gift of prophecy.

In contrast to the inexperienced Christian, there are other prophetic people who are deliberately bizarre. Unlike the beginner, these Christians are more neurotic than nervous. As previously stated, they are just plain weird and must be dealt with firmly and openly. If they exhibit weirdness in a church meeting, they must be addressed and challenged publicly. If they refuse this correction, they must be marked as being rebellious and without discipline.

In all instances where weirdness is displayed, correction must follow. However, it is not always necessary to correct weird people in a harsh manner. Sometimes you can apply the proper correction by employing clever or humorous tactics—which can be just as effective as a severe rebuke. If applied correctly, these tactics can take the sharp edge off a strained atmosphere. Ultimately you get the same results minus the mess created by a cold, calculated rebuke.

A few years ago I heard a good example of correction through humor. It all began in a particular church where prophetic ministry was both taught and encouraged. It seemed that in every meeting three or four people would stand up to give a word of prophecy. In spite of warnings from the pastor concerning wayward prophecies, someone would speak a word that made absolutely no sense. Not wanting to discourage those who possessed a legitimate gift of prophecy, the leaders chose to tolerate this weirdness for a season of time. They hoped that things would eventually get better.

Finally, when their hopes diminished and their patience failed, the elders called a meeting to initiate a plan of action. The plan was simple: The next time someone gave a weird prophecy, it would be addressed immediately. They prayed that God would give them a creative way to neutralize the weirdness without bringing offense to others who were truly prophetic.

The following week, someone stood up in the next meeting and began to prophesy. In a mystical tone of voice this person declared, "Thus saith the Lord: 'I have placed a table before you. I have put a plate on the table and a hammer on the plate. Yea, there is also a fork on the table and a spider crawling on the tablecloth.' " A hush fell over the church. With great expectation, everyone sat on the edge of their seats awaiting the interpretation of the prophecy. They mused: *What could it mean? Did the plate represent God's provision? Was the hammer a type of the Word? Was the spider the devil? And what about the fork? Did it speak of communion or warfare?* No one was really sure.

Finally, one of the elders who was present in the previous meeting, slowly stood to his feet and approached the microphone. With a grin on his face he said, "This is the interpretation of the prophecy. Take the hammer and break the plate. Take the fork and kill the spider. Turn the table over and, by all means, rebuke the person who gave this prophecy."

Needless to say, that was the end of prophetic weirdness in that particular church. The next time an opportunity was made for prophecy, people were a bit more careful with their words. They knew that if they were to give a weird prophecy, it would be met by an even weirder interpretation. As for the leaders of the church, they had learned to fight fire with fire.

User-Friendly Prophetic

Prophetic weirdness is usually symptomatic of a much deeper problem. Often, *people who act weirdly do so because they have a false concept of spirituality.* The real root of their problem is embedded in the belief that being spiritual means being unreal, unnatural, and inhuman. Since they have not learned to be *naturally supernatural*, they are prone to express a fake spirituality, which is accompanied by bizarre behavior. As a result, they and their ministries are not compatible or user-friendly.

Several other misconceptions also prevent believers from being user-friendly. One of these is the idea that we are called to be *deep*. Many Christians equate this so-called spiritual depth with obscure utterances, mystical revelations, and hard-to-understand visions. In fact, a few of these believers are so *deep* that they make absolutely no sense to anyone but themselves. As one sarcastic preacher said, "We have become so deep that even God has trouble understanding our revelation."

Why have we shrouded our ministries with heavy revelations, abstract analogies, and deep sayings? Why do we feel we have to act deep and mystical in order to appear spiritual? And, why have we become so mystical? The answer is clear: We have departed from the simplicity that is found in Christ Jesus. In an attempt to

> **The art of true spiritual ministry is the ability to take complex issues and make them simple. Therefore, we must try to keep it simple, speaking the language of life, rather than the language of religion.**

impress people, we have taken the simple things of God and made them hard to understand. We have failed to learn that the art of true spiritual ministry is the ability to take complex issues and make them simple.

By way of illustration, the ministry of Jesus was characterized by His ability to decode spiritual mysteries. He constantly converted the deep things of God into teaching that was understandable to the masses. He made His ministry user-friendly with the use of parables and stories about fishing and farming. Although He possessed a great depth of understanding, He knew that to reach simple people, He must speak on their level.

As His disciples, we would be wise to follow our Lord's method of ministry. If we desire to connect with the common person, then we must come down from our spiritual high horses and meet the people where they live. Like our Master, we must be approachable, and our ministries must be accessible and down-to-earth. We must try to keep it simple, speaking the language of life rather than the language of religion. Otherwise, we will never be able to relate prophetically to a generation who is looking for user-friendly churches and ministries.

User-Friendly Principles

No two ministries are exactly the same in style and method. We are all unique in personality and distinct in our expression of God. In spite of this diversity, however, a number of basic guidelines can be applied to all who operate in the prophetic. The following is a list of these user-friendly principles:

1. Speak audibly. For the sake of others, don't whisper or mumble.
2. Don't scream. Neither God nor His Church is deaf!
3. Avoid speaking swiftly. Fast talkers are hard to understand.
4. Don't be lengthy. When you ramble on, people lose interest.
5. Don't repeat someone else's word. Redundancy is not always confirmation.

6. Speak in harmony with the atmosphere of the meeting. Don't contradict the flow of the Holy Spirit.
7. Beware of speaking harsh judgment or condemnation. Always try to encourage!
8. Don't monopolize a meeting. Give other people a chance to speak!
9. Keep it simple. Don't try to be deep or mystical!
10. Stick to the point. Don't try to cover too many issues.
11. Don't mimic others. Be yourself!
12. Be direct. Avoid mystical illustrations whenever possible.
13. Avoid disruptive mannerisms. Don't be theatrical.
14. Speak calmly. Don't hype the audience.
15. Develop your own speaking style. Avoid exclusive use of King James vernacular.
16. Don't speak from anger or hurt. Only speak the mind of the Lord.
17. Don't come across as super-spiritual. Haughtiness will limit your effectiveness.
18. Speak with humility. Remember, pride comes before a fall.
19. Don't speak first if you are a novice. Let those who are mature set the pace.
20. Be willing to have your words tested. You are not beyond error.

Solution to Prophetic Weirdness

What is the solution for prophetic weirdness? The answer is obvious: We need to grow up in Christ. We need to let go of our tendencies toward prophetic weirdness and begin to embrace normalcy. In the same way that a child overcomes his childish idiosyncrasies by growing up into maturity, we, too, can overcome our abnormal behavior by growing up in Christ. Like the apostle Paul, we, too, must put away childish behavior and act like spiritual adults (see 1 Cor. 13:11).

If spiritual maturity serves as the primary antidote for much of the weirdness surrounding immature prophetic people, then how do we achieve such a goal? And, can we reach a place of maturity that will allow us to minister effectively to the Church? In the next chapter we will answer this question.

Chapter Fourteen

propHetic maturity

Christian maturity denotes a state of being where one is complete in God, thoroughly developed, and fully grown. This maturity reflects being responsible beyond duty, bearing the burdens of others, giving more than you receive, loving more than you are loved, going the extra mile with your brother, endeavoring to keep the unity of the Spirit, and esteeming others better than yourself.

In First Corinthians 13:11 (RSV), maturity is characterized by the words of a great apostle who declared, "When I was a child, I spoke like a child, I thought like a child, I reasoned like a child; when I became a man, I gave up childish ways." The implication of this verse is that we, as Christians, are called to exchange a lifestyle of immaturity for one of maturity. As a result

We are not born mature, nor at any point in life do we receive the gift of instant maturity. On the contrary, maturity is developed over a period of time...line upon line, precept upon precept.

of this interchange, pride is replaced with purity, ignorance with wisdom, lust with love, selfishness with selflessness, and impatience with patience. This is the essence of spiritual maturation.

Undoubtedly, maturity is the obvious goal for every Christian. Yet, we must understand that maturity does not come to us overnight. We are not born mature, nor at any point in life do we receive the gift of instant maturity. On the contrary, maturity is developed over a period of time. It is a process where we develop "precept upon precept, line upon line" (Is. 28:10). And, in this process of development, we are privileged to grow up in Christ, being "...changed into the same image from glory to glory, even as by the Spirit of the Lord" (2 Cor. 3:18). For some, this can happen in a matter of years; for others it could take a lifetime.

We only need to look at the world around us to illustrate this point. For instance, everything in God's world matures in one fashion or another. Whether it be plants, animals, trees, or people, all of creation begins in infancy and reaches forward to a plateau of perfection. The lion is born small and helpless, hardly able to see or walk. Yet, through a process of growth, he becomes a strong, majestic animal often referred to as the *king of the beasts*. Likewise, a tree begins as an insignificant little seed but eventually matures to the point where it's capable of producing fruit and shade.

The same is true of Christian maturity. In Isaiah 61:3, believers are referred to as being "trees of righteousness, the planting of the Lord." In Psalm 80:15, David refers to the Church as God's "vineyard." Jesus also declared in John 15:5, "I am the vine, ye are the branches: He that abideth in Me, and I in him, the same bringeth forth much fruit...."

Like the tree and the vine, we must submit to God's growth process. We must learn to tolerate the uncertainties associated with Christian development, weather the storms of life, and endure the harsh realities of spiritual winters. To survive this difficult process, we must sink our roots deep into the soil of God's Kingdom and commit ourselves to the process of "abiding in the

Vine." As a result, we will grow strong in the Lord, develop Christian character, and bear an abundance of fruit.

Charisma or Character?

Christians who aspire to operate in prophetic ministry should learn three important truths. First, your gift does not make you mature. Next, the measure of your spiritual gift should not exceed the measure of your spiritual fruit. Finally, *charisma is never an adequate substitute for character.*

These three truths are clearly seen in Paul's exhortation to the Corinthian church. As a spiritual father, the apostle praised the believers for their knowledge and gifts by saying, "...In every way you were enriched in Him with all speech and all knowledge...so that you are not lacking in any spiritual gift..." (1 Cor. 1:5-7 RSV).

Two chapters later, Paul's compliment seems to fade into the severity of a stinging rebuke. He states, "But I, brethren, could not address you as spiritual men, but as men of the flesh, as babes in Christ....for you are still of the flesh. For while there is jealousy and strife [immaturity] among you, are you not of the flesh, and behaving like ordinary men?" (1 Cor. 3:1-3 RSV).

> Today's Church is filled with believers who possess Bible knowledge and spiritual gifts but are devoid of Christian character. These prophets are more concerned about character than charisma.

What is being implied in Paul's exhortation? Was he double-minded in his evaluation of the Corinthian church? Was he confused or possibly demented? Of course not. He was only drawing attention to the dichotomy that existed within the lives of these early believers. As indicated, the Corinthians excelled in the nine gifts of the Spirit—tongues, interpretation of tongues, prophecy, etc. However, they were lacking in the development and expression of the nine fruits of the Spirit, especially long-suffering, gentleness, kindness, and meekness.

Much like the Corinthians, we, too, are "ever learning, and never able to come to the knowledge of the truth" (2 Tim. 3:7). In reality, today's Church is filled with believers who possess Bible knowledge and spiritual gifts but are devoid of Christian character. Many of these Christians are able to preach, prophesy, perform miracles, and heal the sick; however, because their gift greatly exceeds their fruit, their lives and ministries are in jeopardy. When they stand before Jesus on judgment day, they will ask the question, "Lord, Lord, did we not prophesy in Your name, and cast out demons in Your name, and do many mighty works in Your name?" The Lord will answer, "I never knew you; depart from Me, you evil doers" (Mt. 7:22-23 RSV).

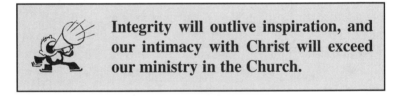

Integrity will outlive inspiration, and our intimacy with Christ will exceed our ministry in the Church.

For this reason, the Lord is raising up a new breed of prophetic people today. These prophets will be more concerned about character than charisma. They will never allow their gift to outshine their fruit. Nor will they confuse talent with maturity. Most importantly, integrity will outlive inspiration, and their intimacy with Christ will exceed their ministry in the Church.

Possessing Maturity

It's one thing to confess maturity and yet another thing to possess it. For example, a child may declare that he is an adult a thousand times a day. Until he actually grows up, though, he convinces no one but himself. Regardless of his relentless confession, reality dictates that he is still a child in every sense of the word. On the other hand, when the child does reach maturity, there is no longer a need to boast about it. Everyone knows he is an adult, not because he says so, but because he looks and acts like an adult. Through growth, he has become what he once confessed.

Jesus said in Matthew 12:33 (RSV), "The tree is known by its fruit." In plain language, a tree is defined by what it produces, not by the name given to it. To illustrate this truth, you can plant a tree in your backyard and tell your neighbors that you now have an apple tree. However, if the tree doesn't produce apples, all the words in the world will not convince them that it's a real apple tree. Yet, if the tree bears apples, you will not have to make a single statement about the nature of the tree. Your neighbors will know it is an apple tree, not because you declare it, but because the fruit speaks for itself.

The same is true of prophetic maturity today. It is not what you say but what you are that makes the real difference. If you truly are a seasoned prophet, you won't have to confess it to the Church. It is not necessary to wear a neon sign around your neck declaring your office, nor is it beneficial to hand out business cards introducing yourself as "God's Prophet." All that's required are the works of a prophet and the fruit that follows. By simply being what God has called you to be, the Church will recognize your prophetic office and respond to it.

> **It is not what you say but what you are that makes the real difference. If you have to convince people that you are a prophet, you have most likely demonstrated that you are not a prophet.**

Therefore, if you have to convince people that you are a prophet, you have most likely demonstrated that you are not a prophet. For instance, Jesus was the greatest prophet of all time and functioned as a prophet to the nation of Israel. Yet, when it came to titles, He merely referred to Himself as the *Son of Man.* His desire to be known as the Father's Son seemed to be more important than bearing the title of *prophet.* Consequently, other people recognized and proclaimed His prophetic office. Such was the case in John 4:19 when the Samaritan woman said to Him, "Sir, I perceive that Thou art a prophet."

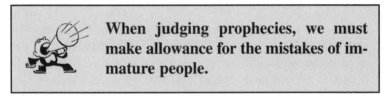

When judging prophecies, we must make allowance for the mistakes of immature people.

Timing

*...Who then is the faithful and wise steward, whom his master will set over his household, to give them their portion of food **at the proper time**?* (Luke 12:42 RSV)

Timing is a crucial aspect of prophetic maturity. Proper timing is absolutely essential for the delivery of a prophetic word. If your timing is right, you can integrate fresh revelation into people's lives with little difficulty. Like water falling on dry ground, a word in season has the potential to refresh the spiritual landscape of the Body of Christ. On the other hand, if your timing is wrong, you may encounter problems in the delivery of the most basic truth.

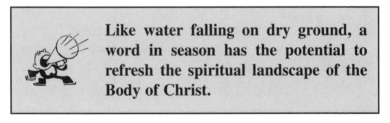

Like water falling on dry ground, a word in season has the potential to refresh the spiritual landscape of the Body of Christ.

As an example, a prophetic word out of season is like a musical note out of sequence. A single, solitary musical note sounds beautiful when played by itself. However, if the note is presented at the wrong time, it can be disruptive to the harmony and to the flow of a song. In the same way, a word of prophecy may be valid and pure within itself but counterproductive when spoken out of season.

Futhermore, just because a word is true doesn't mean that a person is spiritually ready to receive it. In light of this concept, we who are prophetic must learn to deliver truth in the right sequence at the right time. By doing so, we will not be guilty of creating undue stress and discomfort for those who are incapable of handling truth out of season. Like the wise steward in Luke 12:42, we will know when to give them their portion of food at the proper time. Proverbs 15:23b also teaches, "a word spoken in due season, how good is it."

Some years ago, I was asked to minister to a group of upcoming leaders in a particular church. Before I began, the pastor of that church requested that one of his young men who was prophetic minister beside me. The pastor explained that he had a desire to expose the young man to a different flow of prophetic ministry. I agreed and briefly instructed my new partner about the basics of prophetic protocol. Shortly afterward, we began to prophesy over those who were designated to receive ministry. Everything was fine until we came to a gentleman whom we will call Bill.

When I began to focus on Bill, I perceived he had a high calling upon his life. I immediately saw the enormous potential of his ministry and the spiritual gifts that God desired to give him. At the same time I was also aware of his immaturity in the areas of pride and self-promotion. In light of this, the Holy Spirit impressed me that divulging any kind of revelation concerning this man's future ministry, no matter how true, could be counterproductive to the present work of God in his life.

The Spirit continued to instruct me that my prophetic perception about the potential of Bill's ministry was accurate, but the timing for such a word was premature. So I simply prayed for the gentleman and started to move to the next person. At this time the young man who was assisting me turned to Bill and began to prophesy the exact same thing that the Holy Spirit had restricted me from saying. The young man clearly detailed Bill's calling and future ministry, holding nothing back.

Needless to say, everyone in the room was excited about the prophecy. Bill was elated beyond words and the young man who gave the prophecy was now beaming with delight. However, I was saddened by the negative implications of a right word spoken out of season. Knowing what God had shown me about Bill's character, I was sure that the fulfillment of his calling had been jeopardized by a premature prophecy. Bill would probably spend the rest of his life wrestling with spiritual pride. Truth out of season would become his enemy, not his friend.

Was the young man mistaken about the prophecy he gave? Did he misinterpret the purpose of God for Bill's life? I believe God had truly called Bill to a spectacular ministry; however, the revelation of his calling should have been kept secret until such time that Bill could have humbly received it. It was apparent that the young man had tapped into a vein of prophetic truth, but by telling Bill everything he saw, he was more of a hindrance than a help. He made the mistake of applying knowledge without wisdom.

Watchman Nee, in his book, *The Spiritual Man, Volume I* (pages 162-163), addressed this problem of tell-it-all ministry. He clearly describes the actions of believers who are unable to keep their mouths shut. Although he targets Christians in general, the following can also apply to those who flow in prophetic ministry. He begins by saying:

> "Some Christians who are indeed soulish find special delight in helping others. Since they have not yet reached maturity, they do not know how to give food at the proper time. This does not mean these do not have knowledge; actually, they have too much. Upon discovering any improper element or when told of some difficulty, they immediately assume the role of senior believer, eager to help with what limited insight they have. They pour forth scriptural teachings and experiences of saints in lavish

abundance. They are inclined to tell all they know, nay, perhaps more than they know, now reaching into the realm of supposition. These 'senior' believers exhibit, one after another, everything which has been stored in their minds, without at all inquiring whether those to whom they speak really have such a need or can absorb so much teaching in one session. They are like Hezekiah who opened all his storehouses and showed off all his treasures."

I believe Watchman Nee was right about this issue. Spiritual maturity is not defined by what you know but by what you do with the knowledge you have. Likewise, in regard to prophecy, it is often a greater act of maturity to remain silent than to speak a word out of season.

I once heard another wise man named Paul Cain say, *"A prophet is known on earth by what he sees and says, while a prophet is known in Heaven by what he sees and doesn't say."* What an incredible thought! If we believe this is true, then believers who hear from God must learn to keep certain things to themselves. They must keep a guard on their lips at all times, speaking only that which is permitted by God. Otherwise, the Lord will not trust them with secrets relating to people and their problems.

Compassion

One of the most crucial aspects of prophetic ministry is compassion. Without this godly attribute, a prophet is nothing more than an indifferent oracle, methodically speaking forth correction, direction, and judgment without concern for the feelings of others. Like a computer, he may be able to spit out information that he has received but lacks the ability to apply this knowledge with discretion—or present it in a manner appropriate to the need at hand. He coldly pronounces and denounces without feeling responsible for the consequences of his word. His failure to develop a mature love for the Church often prompts him to speak corrective words rather than words of consolation.

On the contrary, the prophet who truly possesses godly compassion will always attempt to season his words with grace, hope, and kindness. As one who commands the prophetic office, he has the right to rebuke and correct the people of God, but he will use this privilege only as a last resort, not as a first response. This prophet's goal is not to malign the Church by passing judgment, but to defend it through prayer and intercession, in hope of restraining the wrath of God. When God does give him an irreversible word of judgment—like Jeremiah, the weeping prophet—he will not deliver the prophecy until it has been thoroughly bathed in his own tears.

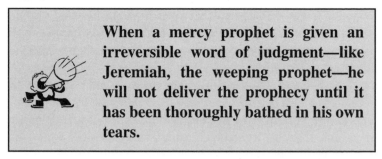

When a mercy prophet is given an irreversible word of judgment—like Jeremiah, the weeping prophet—he will not deliver the prophecy until it has been thoroughly bathed in his own tears.

Compelled by compassion, the mercy prophet will always choose hope over hopelessness, intercession over destruction, and mercy over judgment. His compassion for the people of God will drive him to the prayer closet instead of the pulpit. In an attempt to intercede for those who are subject to the wrath of God, he will wrestle with the Almighty, relentlessly and unashamedly.

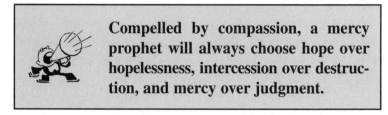

Compelled by compassion, a mercy prophet will always choose hope over hopelessness, intercession over destruction, and mercy over judgment.

Moses, a Mercy Prophet

The Bible gives numerous examples of mature prophets who are characterized by their compassion and mercy, which exceeded their desire to condemn the Church. In Exodus 32:9-14 (TLB) the prophet Moses contended with God on behalf of the children of Israel, whom the Lord called, "a stubborn, rebellious lot." When God's "anger" was blazing against them, Moses begged, "Turn away from this terrible evil You are planning against Your people! Remember Your promise to Your servants...." So, the Lord changed His mind and spared them. Moses interceded for the people of Israel, and God kept them from certain death.

Like Moses, we must also operate in a higher realm of prophetic ministry than rebuke and judgment. Without exception, we should be priests first, prophets second. If we are commanded to speak judgment, we must understand that when God pronounces judgment, He often seeks a man to stand in the gap, to intercede as a priest against the execution of that judgment.

Final Conclusion

As we come to the end of this book, I want to review several points that are critical to the issue of prophetic maturity. First, prophetic maturity embodies much more than dreams, visions, deep revelations, the ability to prophesy, and the privilege of discerning and judging the Body of Christ. These things may be necessary for the equipping of the saints but are pale in comparison to the value of comfort, encouragement, and compassionate intercession. Therefore, as priestly prophets, we must endeavor "to comfort all that mourn...to give unto them beauty for ashes, the oil of joy for mourning..." (Is. 61:2-3).

Next, we can either whip the saints or equip the saints with the gift of prophecy. We can tear down or build up, encourage or discourage. We can spend our spiritual gifts to buy self-acclaim

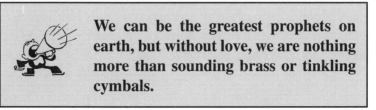

We can be the greatest prophets on earth, but without love, we are nothing more than sounding brass or tinkling cymbals.

and popularity, or we can spend our lives as a token of love and intercession for the Church. Whatever the choice, remember, *we are not true prophets of God until we can first profit God's Kingdom.*

Finally, the real test of prophetic ministry doesn't lie in the greatness of our spiritual gift, but in the quality of our spirit. In this context, a pure heart is equal in Kingdom value to that of a pure gift or theology. Moreover, the condition of our heart is just as significant as the condition of our ministry. It's important that we desire spiritual gifts; however, we must understand one vital truth. We can be the greatest prophets on earth, but without love, we are nothing more than sounding brass or tinkling cymbals (see 1 Cor. 13:1).

forty commonly asked questions and answers

1. What is the gift of prophecy?

The New Testament gift of prophecy is one of the nine gifts of the Spirit outlined in First Corinthians 12. Paul further states in this book that one who prophesies speaks to men for edification, exhortation, and consolation. He also declares that the one who prophesies edifies the whole Church (see 1 Cor. 14:3-4).

Strong's Exhaustive Concordance defines *prophecy, prophesy* and *prophesying* as "predicting or foretelling events; to divine; to speak under inspiration; an inspired speaker; a poet." In *Scribner's Dictionary of the Bible*, W.T. Davison, describing *prophecy*, states that "The Hebrew word nabi, which is used over 300 times in the Old Testament, was long associated with a root word meaning 'bubble up'" (page 757). This concept of bubbling up presents a word picture that conveys an essential truth about prophecy: namely, that prophecy often springs forth or bubbles up out of the resident anointing that lies within every New Testament believer.

2. Is prophecy biblical?

The Bible is a collection of written prophecies. From Genesis to Revelation, every word is bathed with prophetic implications. The Bible also declares that the testimony of Jesus is the spirit of prophecy (see Rev. 19:10). Since the words *prophecy, prophesy,* and *prophesied* are used more than 160 times in the King James Bible, it is not surprising that the apostle Paul also instructs us to "…desire spiritual gifts, but rather that ye may prophesy" (1 Cor. 14:1).

3. Is prophecy for today?

The Scripture declares that Jesus is the same yesterday, today, and forever—and that the gifts and callings of God are without repentance (see Heb. 13:8; Rom. 11:29). In light of this truth, I believe our Lord is unwavering in His commitment to endow us with spiritual gifts. If He gave prophecy to the New Testament Church, we, too, can expect to receive the same gift. Peter confirms this truth in Acts 2:17. "…In the last days, saith God, I will pour out of My Spirit upon all flesh: and *your sons and your daughters shall prophesy….*"

4. The Bible states that prophecy shall cease. When shall this be?

Paul teaches us in First Corinthians 13:8-10, "…Whether there be prophecies, they shall fail; whether there be tongues, they shall cease; whether there be knowledge, it shall vanish away. For we know in part, and *we prophesy in part.* But when that which is perfect is come, then that which is in part shall be done away."

According to these Scriptures, prophecy will vanish at the coming of that which is perfect. Many Bible teachers are convinced that this has already happened. They argue that the canonization of Scripture, which resulted in our Bible, was the perfect revelation that replaces our need for further prophecy. If this holds true, then according to First Corinthians 13:8, both tongues and knowledge also would have passed away centuries ago. Since we know that this premise is false, one can only assume that Paul was referring to the Second Coming of Jesus. Indeed, our Savior is the Perfect One, and once He returns to earth, He will obviously overshadow all tongues, knowledge, and prophecy. Until then, Scripture exhorts us to actively use the prophetic gift to build up His Bride, the Church.

5. Should the one who prophesies be a Bible teacher or theologian?

God does not prize ignorance. The right type of biblical training *can* add to and enrich one's prophetic gift. On the other hand, highly educated believers are often lifted up in the pride of their learning and lean upon their intellect rather than on the inspiration of the Holy Spirit. Due to this error, God often uses the weak and uneducated to confound the wise. He also delights in revealing His mind to babes and hiding it from the proud.

6. Is the sole purpose of prophecy to foretell the future?

Although the gift of prophecy is used to predict the future, it is also used to speak words of exhortation, edification, and comfort. For example, the prophet Samuel could look into the future and speak of things which were yet to come. On the other hand, the Bible portrays King Saul prophesying under the inspiration of the Holy Spirit, but gives no indication that he foretold future events.

It is also recorded in the New Testament that, Jesus, John the revelator, Agabus, and the apostle Paul foretold future events. However, the Corinthian church was also exhorted by Paul to prophesy edification, exhortation, and comfort—a form of prophecy that was seemingly without a predictive element.

7. Who can prophesy?

In First Corinthians 12:11, Paul teaches that the Holy Spirit distributes the gifts of the Spirit to every man "severally as He will." However, he later encouraged the whole Church to "desire spiritual gifts, but rather that ye may prophesy" (1 Cor. 14:1). In light of these Scriptures, the gift of prophecy may not initially be given to everyone—but is available to all those who earnestly desire it. This is true for both sheep and shepherd, educated and uneducated, male and female, child and adult. All who have a heart to encourage the Church may prophesy.

8. Should prophecy be spoken in the first, second, or third person?

The way prophecy should be spoken is optional. It can either be first, second, or third person, depending upon the choice of the person speaking. For example:

    a. First Person: "I am merciful, saith the Lord."

    b. Second Person: "The Lord is merciful."

    c. Third Person: "The Lord says He is merciful."

9. Should one stand when prophesying?

There are no absolute rules whether one should sit or stand when prophesying. However, if others are sitting in a meeting, you may want to stand up to indicate that the Spirit is upon you and that you are looking for permission to speak. Whatever the posture, remember that it is the anointing that qualifies your gift—not your style, personality, or body language.

10. Should Scripture be quoted when prophesying?

The answer is twofold. First, prophecy should always complement Scripture and in no instance be contrary to it. In which case, it's beneficial to memorize and express the Scriptures that support what is being prophesied. Last, it isn't necessary for all prophetic words to be couched in Scripture. Remember, merely quoting Scripture isn't always synonymous with prophecy.

11. Is it right to pray for and covet the gift of prophecy?

In First Corinthians 14:1, Paul exhorts us to "desire spiritual gifts, but rather that ye may prophesy." In verse 31, he further teaches that "...ye may all prophesy." In verse 39, we are also told to "covet" (be jealous for) prophecy. However, our pursuit of prophecy must be founded on a right motive. We must covet prophecy for the edification, encouragement, and comfort of the Church—not for the purpose of self gain or power.

12. Is the gift of prophecy greater than the gift of tongues?

Paul writes in First Corinthians 14:5 "...greater is he that prophesieth than he that speaketh with tongues." This order of priority is significant in two ways. First, Paul declares that a prophetic utterance is greater in usefulness than that of an utterance of tongues. For example, a person who is suicidal would benefit more from a prophetic word spoken to him in his own language, than from an unintelligible utterance in an unknown tongue. Second, prophecy is given for the edification of others; the gift of tongues is given for building up the person giving it. Therefore, if we believe that it is more blessed to give than to receive, we must recognize that the use of prophecy in a public setting is greater than the use of tongues, unless there is an interpretation of the message of tongues.

13. Is prophecy the greatest gift?

Although prophecy plays a prominent role in Scripture, the gift of prophecy does not excel in usefulness over all the other gifts. In my opinion, the greatest gift is the one which meets the greatest need at the moment. For instance, a person dying of a dread disease would benefit more from someone who has the gift of healing than from one who has the gift of prophecy (except when the gift of prophecy is used to complement the gift of healing and heighten a person's faith in God's power to heal him).

14. Should prophetic words ever be written and delivered in written form?

The greater part of Scripture is prophecy in written form. Many of the Old and New Testament prophets and some of the New Testament prophets recorded their prophecies, which were saved for future generations. Although our prophecies will never equal Scripture, it is beneficial to write out a prophecy—even if we intend to give it orally. An additional benefit for putting one's prophecies into writing is that once we have them in written form, we can do research and compare them to Scripture. This enables us to search for any hidden symbolism the prophecies might have and to receive a more complete grasp of their meaning.

15. Should prophecy be given in the presence of unbelievers?

Although some disagree, Scripture places no limits on where to prophesy. In the Old Testament, Saul prophesied in the open. Eldad and Medad also prophesied in the camp (see Num. 11:26). In the New Testament, Paul indicates that unbelievers will fall on their faces and confess their sins when prophecy is uttered in a church meeting (see 1 Cor. 14:24-25).

16. Should I deliver a prophetic word immediately after I receive it?

Proper timing is essential to the delivery and effectiveness of a prophetic word. Upon receiving a prophetic word, dream, or vision from God, it isn't always necessary to immediately release it. Many times we need to pray over our revelation for further clarification, for faith to accurately deliver the word, and for the reception and cooperation of the person receiving the prophecy. Remember, the spirit of the prophet is subject to the prophet. This means we have control over our own spirits and can withhold or release what God gives to us.

17. Is it proper for more than one person to prophesy in a church service?

Paul taught the Corinthian church to prophesy in order, one person at a time (see 1 Cor. 14:31). The purpose of this instruction was to limit the confusion in church meetings. He taught that although two or more may sense the same anointing, have the same message, and feel motivated to speak, only one should prophesy at a time. The others should listen and then judge the validity of the prophecy.

18. Is it wise for a pastor to appoint only one person within the congregation to prophesy?

The Bible strongly encourages all Christians to prophesy. However, certain people excel in the use of the gift of prophecy.

Therefore, when a pastor recognizes an advanced gift of prophecy operating in a believer, he might be more inclined to place a higher degree of trust in the validity of that person's prophetic insight. As a result, he may honor the prophetic gifting and make frequent use of it. Although this is not necessarily wrong, pastors must also learn how to receive from believers who are less proficient in this gifting.

19. Can the exercise of the gift of prophecy be stifled in a church service?

The writer of First Thessalonians 5:19-20 warns us to "quench not the Spirit" and "despise not prophesyings." In light of these scriptural warnings, it's apparent that the spirit of prophecy is subject to the atmosphere created by believers. Where there is faith, desire, and respect for prophecy, the Spirit will respond by releasing prophetic expressions which emanate from the heart of God. Where there is doubt, unbelief, and animosity toward the prophetic, prophecy will be limited, if not completely quenched. In Mark 6:4-5 we see that Jesus' own ministry was limited by those around Him. "But Jesus said unto them, A prophet is not without honour, but in his own country, and among his own kin, and in his own house. And He could there do no mighty work, save that He laid His hands upon a few sick folk, and healed them."

20. If a pastor stops me from prophesying in his church when I feel I have a word from God, would I be in disobedience to God if I submit to the pastor's wishes?

You're not sinning by cooperating with or submitting to the authority God has placed over an assembly of believers. If the pastor is wrong in rejecting your ministry, God will deal with him. If the pastor is sincere in his heart but mistaken about you and your gifting, God will bless him anyway and eventually teach him to better discern the Body of Christ. In the meantime, God won't require you to interrupt or take over his service. Remember, it is always better to submit to godly authority than to undermine it.

21. How does one begin to receive prophetic words from God?

All Christians are unique in personality, nature, and spirit. None of us receive or hear from God in exactly the same way. Although some hear the audible voice of the Lord, others receive an inward witness of the Spirit in their hearts. Some have dreams and others see visions. Some have Scriptures quickened in their minds; others receive mental pictures. Many prophetic people will feel different sensations in their bodies, such as burning and shaking, while others feel nothing more than a keen sense of awareness, which emerges out of the depths of their spirits.

22. Can people who have a valid gift of prophecy make a mistake and still continue to grow in their gifting without being labeled a false prophet?

New Testament believers have been given the latitude to prophetically express the heart of God in our own words. Therefore, when one is prophesying, one's temperament, personality, doctrinal ideas, and level of maturity play a vital role in the delivery of prophecy. As a result, mistakes can be made if the speaker fails to properly interpret the mind of the Spirit. Nervousness or inexperience will also add to this margin of error. The apostle Paul states, "For we know in part, and we prophesy in part. ...one by one, that all may learn..." (1 Cor. 13:9; 14:31). This supports the proposition that we can grow in our prophetic gifting and still have the freedom to learn from our mistakes. However, the mistakes arise from the speaker, not from the gift. People make mistakes; God cannot err.

23. Will God punish people who prophesy out of their own spirit?

If a Christian is sincere in his heart but immature in his gifting and doesn't know how to yield or appropriate the anointing, God will bear with him for a season until he refines his gift. If your child was hungry and asked you for food in a wrong way or with a poor attitude, would you punish him or let him starve? Of course not! You would feed the child in spite of his speech or approach. The same is true of prophecy. God is neither quick to judge nor punish us for our mistakes or immaturity.

24. Are all dreams prophetic in nature?

Not all dreams convey a real message to the dreamer. Solomon teaches us in Ecclesiastes 5:3 that a number of dreams "...cometh through the multitude of business...." On the other hand, supernaturally inspired dreams often carry a specific message from God, which should be carefully interpreted and applied in our lives. Most of the recorded instances of God speaking to man in the Bible are through dreams and visions. Job states, "In a dream, in a vision of the night, when deep sleep falleth upon men, in slumberings upon the bed; then He openeth the ears of men, and sealeth their instruction" (Job 33:15-16).

25. Is prophecy given exclusively for the benefit of believers?

Scripture indicates that the basic purpose of prophecy is for the edification, exhortation, and comfort of the Church. However, there are instances in the Bible where prophecy was given to unbelievers. In one instance, a prophetic dream from God was given to the Pharaoh of Egypt. As a result, Joseph interpreted the dream (having already interpreted the prophetic dreams of Pharaoh's butler and baker). He was then elevated to the second highest position in Egypt so that he might deliver Israel, the Egyptians, and the surrounding countries from severe famine and drought.

Another Scripture records that the Chaldean king Nebuchadnezzar was also given prophetic dreams (see Dan. 4). A prophet, called Daniel, interpreted those dreams, which ultimately led the king to declare, "Now I Nebuchadnezzar praise and extol and honour the King of heaven..." (Dan. 4:37). Consequently, both of these dreams served as tools of evangelism and salvation at that particular time in history.

26. How do I know that the word I received is from God?

Jesus declared in John 10:4 that His sheep "know His voice." Although mature sheep often hear and recognize their master's voice, that doesn't mean that little lambs are familiar with the Great Shepherd's voice. Therefore, until we are mature enough to rightly discern and identify the voice of our Master, we must test all things that we hear and see. We must not only judge the revelation that we receive but also test the spirit behind the revelation.

27. How are we to judge prophecy?

Judging prophecy is more of a commandment than an option. First Thessalonians 5:21 instructs us to "prove all things; hold fast that which is good." Paul also declares, "But he that is spiritual judgeth all things..." (1 Cor. 2:15). To the Corinthian church he wrote, "Let the prophets speak two or three, and let the other judge" (1 Cor. 14:29).

However, we must not confuse criticism with righteous judgment. Our purpose for judging prophecy is to discern and separate truth from untruth, and spirit from flesh (not to critique the mannerism, method, and personality of the person, which often bleeds through prophetic utterances). In fact, Scripture teaches us that we are to test the spirit, not the mannerisms of the person prophesying (see 1 Jn. 4:1).

28. Is there a particular style or method one should use when prophesying?

There is no set standard, method, mannerism, or behavior required when prophesying. There are some people who are demonstrative by nature, while others are more subdued. Likewise, while some Christians choose to speak loudly and forcefully; others are comfortable speaking in a normal tone of voice.

Whatever the case may be, it's important to reflect upon the words of John the Baptist, who said, "He must increase, but I must decrease" (Jn. 3:30). Like John, we must not draw attention to ourselves when ministering in the prophetic. Our purpose must be to exalt the Lord and to encourage the brethren. Remember, whatever your style, God places His emphasis upon your character and the purity of your word—not upon your personality!

29. Can a person prophesy without the anointing of the Holy Spirit?

There are times when well-meaning Christians give a prophecy without the inspiration of the Holy Spirit. Due to an overzealous spirit, some of these believers are inclined to overstep the maturity level of their gifting and, as a result, speak out of their human spirit, imagination, or intellect. Regardless of their zeal, they are not sinning by speaking out of their immaturity.

30. Can I have the gift of prophecy and not know it?

The Bible often portrays God as a farmer who plants seeds in hopes of reaping a mature crop at a later time. The same is true of the gift of prophecy and other spiritual gifts. Many times these gifts are imparted to us in seed or embryonic form and often lie dormant within our spirit, hidden for an extended period of time beneath the conscious level of our soul. Therefore, we must learn to identify, cultivate, and nurture the gifts given to us and to those whom God has given us influence over. We must learn to see "those things that are not as though they are."

31. Can I have the gift of prophecy and not have love?

Love is a fruit of the Spirit that comes out of godly character. On the other hand, prophecy is a gift of the Spirit given to us by the Holy Spirit, independent of our ability to love. In this regard, Christians may be enriched in knowledge and laden with spiritual gifts, but not possess the love of God.

Such was the case of the believers in Corinth. Paul sharply rebuked these first century Christians for their lack of love. In First Corinthians 13, he declared to them that love was the greatest gift of all. He further indicated that mature believers are characterized by the expression of their gifts through love.

32. Are there different levels of prophetic ministry?

In my opinion, there are four basic levels of prophetic utterance and ministry. The first pertains to the Spirit of prophecy and is a corporate anointing. It falls upon a gathering of believers—enabling those who are not prophets, or those who don't possess the gift of prophecy—to prophesy.

The second level relates to the gift of prophecy and is a resident endowment of the Spirit given to certain believers by the discretion of the Holy Spirit. It is also a resident gift that can be utilized whenever necessary.

The third level incorporates a prophetic mantle and is a ministry function empowered by a strong prophetic anointing resting upon an individual at all times.

The fourth level is the office of prophet, which is a governmental position mentioned in Ephesians 4:11. This is a fivefold ministry function given to the Church for the purpose of bringing revelation, foretelling, rebuking, affirming, encouragement, direction, and ministry confirmation.

33. If I prophesy, does that mean I am a prophet?

Sawing a board or hammering a nail now and then doesn't make one a carpenter. Neither do we become professional race car drivers just because we know how to drive an automobile. One is a lifelong profession requiring commitment, skill, extensive training, dedication, and discipline. The other is an occasional activity, secondary to your life's purpose. This same principle also applies to the prophetic. The fact that you can prophesy doesn't necessarily qualify you for the office of prophet.

34. If I make a mistake in prophesying, does that make me a false prophet?

If a policeman is involved in a case of mistaken identity and arrests the wrong person, does that mean he is a false policeman? If a pastor makes a mistake in counseling one of his flock, does that make him a false shepherd? Of course not! We are all imperfect people and make mistakes now and then. The difference between false and true prophets doesn't always lie in the perfection or accuracy of their prophetic words but in the attitude or motive of their hearts. For example, a false prophet can be accurate in what he says, but wrong in his heart and spirit. On the other hand, a godly prophet can be mistaken in his prophecy but pure in his heart. Which of these do you think God will honor and endorse?

35. Other than speaking prophecy, are there other forms of prophetic expression?

Song, dance, drama, art, and mime have all been used in the Bible as vehicles of prophetic expression. For instance, the Book of Psalms is a collection of prophetic songs written by the psalmist David. Also, in the Book of Exodus, we see Miriam, the sister of Moses, leading the women of Israel in a prophetic song and dance. In addition, the Song of Solomon, which some consider to be one of the most prophetic books in the Bible, was written as a play. The Bible also tells us that many Old Testament prophets, such as Jeremiah and Ezekiel, acted out their prophecies much like a mime would silently act out a story.

36. Is prophecy conditional?

After creating mankind in His image, God granted us a free will and gave us the freedom of choice. In light of this truth, God is reluctant to violate our will in order to bring His purposes to pass in our lives. In that regard, the success and failure of a prophetic utterance spoken over us is contingent upon the will and mental posture of the person receiving the word. By choice, the person either complies with the word, denies its importance, or worse, incurs judgment for disobeying the word that is given.

As an example, in the Old Testament, Israel received a prophetic word that the people would enter into Canaan, the land of promise. However, since they set their hearts against God's word by murmuring and complaining in disobedience, they incurred God's wrath and died in the wilderness, never reaching their destination.

37. Is it ever proper to speak correction and rebuke through prophecy?

Although the primary purpose of the New Testament gift of prophecy is to bring edification, exhortation, and comfort to the Church, there are times when it is necessary to prophesy correction and rebuke. Remember, though, using the prophetic to bring a corrective word or a rebuke is reserved solely for those who operate out of the governmental office of a prophet. Even then, the rebuke should come as a last resort, not as a first response.

38. Can I give direction for believers' lives through a prophetic utterance?

Directional prophecy is a dynamic that is better served by those who minister in the office of a prophet. Occasionally, God will use prophetic believers to give words of direction, such as where to move or where to work. However, this is more of an exception than the rule. Therefore, before you prophesy direction, remember: God will hold you personally responsible for sending His children down the wrong path in life.

39. What are the gifts of the word of knowledge and the word of wisdom? How do they relate to the gift of prophecy?

The word of knowledge is one of the nine gifts of the Spirit outlined in First Corinthians 12. It's the supernatural ability to discern and speak forth things known to others, but, at the time, not known to you. For instance, when this gift operates through believers, they know certain things about total strangers, both past and present. Many times this knowledge includes a *specific word* about sicknesses, family problems, financial status, names, birthdates, and other personal information. This does not reveal new insight to the one receiving ministry. However, his faith and level of expectancy is heightened by hearing a stranger identify specific details about his life.

The gift of the word of wisdom is also one of the nine gifts of the Spirit. It's also a supernatural ability used to discern and speak forth God-breathed wisdom for a particular person or situation. Those who exercise this gift often speak into peoples' lives concerning God's wisdom for their future. In many instances, revelation is given to guide individuals—how and where they are to conduct their lives and with what timing.

The word of knowledge and the word of wisdom are complementary to the gift of prophecy. These gifts seem to flow together in one prophetic stream, making it hard to distinguish one from another. The gift of knowledge and the gift of wisdom are narrow in scope of revelation, while the gift of prophecy is panoramic in scope and vision. Also, the words of knowledge and wisdom are given for the benefit of one believer; whereas, prophecy is given for the benefit of the corporate Church.

40. How do I learn to hear God's voice?

Several truths are central to the dynamic of hearing God's voice. First, God, who is divinely unique, has also made us unique. It is difficult therefore to teach others how to hear from a God who is unique in nature and diverse in expression. Second, depending on the circumstances, God speaks in many different forms—ranging from an audible voice to an inner voice, from dreams to visions, from mental pictures to inner impressions. Third, in spite of how we hear from God, we can become more receptive to His voice and attentive to His ways through prayer, fasting, meditation, worship, and intense scrutiny of the Scripture. Finally, to enhance our ability to hear God's voice, we must begin to commune with God on a daily basis. The more we get to know the Father and walk in fellowship with His Son, Jesus, the better equipped we will be to hear His voice and speak His word.

For further information, please address your correspondence to:

Larry Randolph Ministries
P.O. Box 5058
San Dimas, CA 91773
(909) 599-8067

Destiny Image
New Releases

WORSHIP: THE PATTERN OF THINGS IN HEAVEN
by Joseph L. Garlington.
Joseph Garlington, a favorite Promise Keepers' speaker and worship leader, delves into Scripture to reveal worship and praise from a Heaven's-eye view. Learn just how deep, full, and anointed God intends our worship to be.
Paperback Book, 182p. ISBN 1-56043-195-4 Retail $8.99

WHEN GOD STRIKES THE MATCH
by Dr. Harvey R. Brown, Jr.
A noted preacher, college administrator, and father of an "all-American" family—what more could a man want? But when God struck the match that set Harvey Brown ablaze, it ignited a passion for holiness and renewal in his heart that led him into a head-on encounter with the consuming fire of God.
Paperback Book, 160p. ISBN 0-7684-1000-2 (6" X 9") Retail $8.99

THE LOST ART OF INTERCESSION
by Jim W. Goll.
How can you experience God's anointing power as a result of your own prayer? Learn what the Moravians discovered during their 100-year prayer Watch. They sent up prayers; God sent down His power. Jim Goll, who ministers worldwide through a teaching and prophetic ministry, urges us to heed Jesus' warning to "watch." Through Scripture, the Moravian example, and his own prayer life, Jim Goll proves that "what goes up must come down."
Paperback Book, 182p. ISBN 1-56043-697-2 Retail $8.99

PRAY WITH FIRE
by Guy Chevreau.
How do we pray in the midst of revival? *Pray With Fire!* Dr. Guy Chevreau, of the Toronto Airport Christian Fellowship renewal team, created this inspirational resource for anyone walking in revival's fire. You'll read testimonies of people soaked in God's glory and delve into "fiery" prayers of Spirit-filled people of the past—especially those of the Master, Himself.
Paperback Book, 224p. ISBN 1-56043-698-0 Retail $8.99

Available at your local Christian bookstore.

Internet: http://www.reapernet.com

Prices subject to change without notice.

Exciting titles
by Don Nori

Exciting titles
by Dr. Bill Hamon

APOSTLES, PROPHETS AND THE COMING MOVES OF GOD

Author of the "Prophets" series, Dr. Bill Hamon brings the same anointed instruction in this new series on apostles! Learn about the apostolic age and how apostles and prophets work together. Find out God's end-time plans for the Church!

Paperback Book, 336p. ISBN 0-939868-09-1 Retail $12.99

PROPHETS AND PERSONAL PROPHECY

This book defines the role of a prophet or prophetess and gives the reader strategic guidelines for judging prophecy. Many of the stories included are taken from Dr. Bill's ministry and add that "hands on" practicality that is quickly making this book a best-seller.

Paperback Book, 252p. ISBN 0-939868-03-2 Retail $9.99

PROPHETS, PITFALLS, AND PRINCIPLES

This book shows you how to recognize your hidden "root" problems, and detect and correct character flaws and "weed seed" attitudes. It also can teach you how to discern true prophets using Dr. Hamon's ten M's.

Paperback Book, 238p. ISBN 0-939868-05-9 Retail $9.99

PROPHETS AND THE PROPHETIC MOVEMENT

This sequel to *Prophets and Personal Prophecy* is packed with the same kind of cutting instruction that made the first volume a best-seller. Prophetic insights, how-to's, and warnings make this book essential for the Spirit-filled church.

Paperback Book, 252p. ISBN 0-939868-04-0 Retail $9.99

Available at your local Christian bookstore.

Internet: http://www.reapernet.com